It's the Fed, Stupid

Thomas Mullen

ISBN-13: 978-1-7379245-2-4

For all those, modest and mighty, who produce more than they consume

Contents

CHAPTER 1

WHY ELECTIONS HAVEN'T MATTERED

The 21st century has seen two political movements replace the bipartisan status quo of the century before. The left moved away from the centrist liberalism of the Bill Clinton years to the Occupy Wall Street movement following the 2008 financial crisis. It now marches under the banner of "democratic socialism," championed by two-time presidential candidate Bernie Sanders in the U.S. Senate and "The Squad" in the House of Representatives.

The right rejected the Bush administration's neoconservatism in favor of smaller, more constitutionally limited government during the Tea Party years, electing a

"Freedom Caucus" to Congress beginning in 2010. Now, this same caucus often runs afoul of the economic nationalists of the dominant movement on the American right today, the Make America Great Again (MAGA) movement led by Donald Trump.

Both the democratic socialists and economic nationalists seek roughly the same ends via different means. However, both fail to see the true cause of disproportionate income inequality, the erosion of the middle class, and the concentration of political power in the hands of a billionaire global elite. Rather than "unfettered capitalism," decried by both movements, it is the distinctly anti-capitalist Federal Reserve System that is chiefly responsible for the societal ills they seek to cure.

The title of this book is a play on Bill Clinton operative James Carville's famous instruction to campaign staffers to focus on "the economy, stupid." It was also the title of the first article I ever wrote on politics back in 2008.[1] That article was inspired by the man who later wrote the book, *End the Fed*. Of course, I am talking about Ron Paul, who sought the Republican nomination for president in 2008 and 2012.

Paul did not win the nomination, but he succeeded in drawing much more attention to the Federal Reserve than it had been paid in decades. For the first time, people began to realize the Fed might have something to do with *creating* crises like the 2008 housing meltdown, rather than merely responding to them with policies few people understand.

So popular was criticizing the Fed in 2011 that even Republican presidential candidate Rick Perry tried to get in on the act.

> If this guy [Fed Chairman Ben Bernanke] prints more money between now and the election, I dunno what y'all would do to him in Iowa but we would treat him pretty ugly down in Texas. Printing more money to play politics at this particular time in American history is almost treacherous – or treasonous in my opinion."[2]

As Mr. Hand from *Fast Times at Ridgemont High* might say, "That's very close, Rick." While monetary inflation certainly doesn't meet the constitutional definition of treason, it is very destructive economically. It's also a pretty boring topic for most people, which allows the Fed to evade responsibility for the problems it causes. Politicians are much easier for people to love or hate and get a lot more attention from the media.

Over the past two decades, both major parties have had the opportunity to simultaneously control the White House and both houses of Congress. While the rhetoric has certainly been stormy, it's hard to argue either party changed much. The federal government continued to grow by leaps and bounds under the leadership of both. The national debt exploded from just under $6 trillion at the start of the century to over $28 trillion today.[3]

The power exercised by the government has grown with its spending. During the war on terror, the government claimed the authority to monitor all our communications, financial records, and online activity. Over the past two years, it has seized authority to shut down our businesses, nullify our rental contracts, and even dictate our medical decisions.

These power grabs have all been accomplished by unelected bureaucrats in executive branch agencies, ostensibly under the direction of elected presidents, but for the most part pursuing their agendas regardless of the president's wishes. This is the inevitable result of a federal bureaucracy over four million employees strong.

Those four million include the worldwide standing army the U.S maintains through Democratic and Republican administrations alike. Every once in a while, a war finally ends, as Afghanistan did in 2021. Yet, in 2022, the Department of Defense budget will increase significantly.[4] The U.S. spends more on the military than the next thirteen countries combined.[5] The $28 billion *increase* in U.S. military spending for 2022 is $5 billion more than was *total* 2021 military spending by Canada, which has the 14th largest military in the world.

No government this size could exist merely on the taxes it collects. The one in Washington, D.C. certainly hasn't. That's why it needs the silent, insidious tax of inflation to surreptitiously extract from the people what it could never obtain through the political process.

Meanwhile, the people remain distracted by politicians who make fiery speeches promising mostly inconsequential changes, while the institution that affects their lives most significantly remains unchecked and largely unnoticed.

This book is an attempt to change that. Over the ensuing fourteen years since that first article, I've appealed to every political movement that has come, gone or stayed the same. Whether you've been a Wall Street Occupier, Tea Partier, Bernie Bro, or MAGA conservative, my message has been and remains the same. So, please don't take offense as I attempt the best down home, Louisiana accent a Western New York native can muster and give it to you straight:

It's the Fed, stupid.

CHAPTER 2

THE FEDERAL RESERVE RUNS THE ECONOMY

Originally published May 19, 2015

Janet Yellen told the markets what they wanted to hear today and the indexes rocketed out of negative territory to finish up over 1 %. As usual, speculation abounds on precisely what was in the minds of investors.

Journalists tend to overstate the causal importance of breaking news when the market makes big moves. Often, those moves were predicted months in advance by serious traders and what happened that day had little to do with what the market did. Not true for the Fed's announcements. They do move the markets immediately.

What most people don't know, or at least don't acknowledge, is that the Federal Reserve really runs the entire economy. When the Fed inflates the supply of money and credit, indexes go up, growth occurs and the economy "improves." When it deflates the supply of money and credit, indexes go down, contraction occurs and the economy "slows."

That's really the whole story of the American economy. Think about that for a moment.

It doesn't matter who is president, which party controls Congress or what any of those people do or don't do. Yes, regulations and tax rates have some effect on the economy. Liberals might say more regulation is a good thing, conservatives might say it is bad.

But taxes and regulations haven't really had much effect at all in the past 40 years. Before that, when taxes were at 90%, they mattered, but not when the top rate fluctuates between 35% and 39%. Do the math. It's not that significant.

Regulations haven't changed that much since the New Deal, either. Yes, there was some mild "deregulation" and subsequent "re-regulation." They caused little bumps and bounces, but nothing compared to the wild swings caused by monetary policy.

In reality, what elected officials have done since 1971, when the U.S. dollar became a completely fiat currency, has had about as much effect on the economy as a blow dryer in a hurricane. Point it with the wind and it makes the wind blow infinitesimally faster. Point it against the wind and it makes the wind blow infinitesimally slower. Either way, the difference is negligible.

Once you understand this, most political narratives about the economy become fairy tales. Liberals credit Bill Clinton with "managing the economy" well during the boom years of the 1990's. Conservatives say it was that Republican Congress.

Neither Clinton and nor Congress had anything to do with it. They were the blow dryers. The 90's economy was really just a tech bubble blown up by the Fed with inflation that burst in 2000 when the Fed tightened. Clinton and the Republican Congress were both in office for the whole time.

Neither did anything significant to cause the boom or the bust. It was all the Fed.

No one really disputes the Fed's role. American voters just don't draw the obvious conclusions. They continue to talk about presidents or Congress as if they significantly affect the economy, when in reality they don't. At least they don't anymore.

This couldn't have been truer than for George W. Bush, who did almost nothing that affected the economy, other than sign Sarbanes-Oxley. Yet, Bush gets credit from Republicans for a "Bush Boom" and blame from Democrats for the housing meltdown.

Those, too, were all the Fed. The Fed blew up the housing bubble with monetary inflation in an attempt to stimulate recovery after its tech bubble burst. It popped the housing bubble it created when it tightened. That's what caused the Bush Boom and the Bush Bust. Bush himself was just along for the ride.

Now, we have market indexes at an all-time high and an economy that has supposedly "recovered." As usual, the president takes credit for all of this. If the crash comes on his watch, he'll take all of the blame. But, like Bush, Obama is just along for the ride. There really is no cause/effect relationship between anything he's done and what we're seeing in the Dow or S&P 500 indexes.

What we're really seeing are the results of unprecedented monetary inflation by the Fed, holding interest rates at an unprecedented low (near zero) for an unprecedented period of time (over six years).

That anyone can even comment on the economy without acknowledging the effect of this Fed activity is surreal. For six straight years, it has literally just printed up money and handed it out to banks, acquiring those worthless, mortgage backed securities at face value, even though they couldn't be sold on the market at any price.

In 2008, the Fed's balance sheet was $800 billion. It's now $4.5 trillion. It's staggering.

Nothing done by Obama or any legislator, Republican or Democrat, has had any significant effect on the economy compared to this tidal wave of money and credit.

Think about what this means. Before virtually every election, American voters say the economy is their most important concern. They vote for the people whose policies they believe will bring jobs and prosperity.

But they're kidding themselves. It doesn't matter if they replace all 535 Congressmen and the president in a single election. It's going to affect the economy about as much as 536 blow dryers can change the direction of the wind in a Florida hurricane.

We can argue whether it's a good thing or a bad thing that a small, unelected group of bankers is in complete control of all meaningful economic outcomes. But let's at least face the reality that they are.

CHAPTER 3

WHAT ABOUT THE TRUMP BOOM?

Even those who agree with everything in the previous chapter get amnesia when their candidate of choice gets elected. In President Trump's case, even the candidate himself got amnesia.

During his 2016 presidential campaign, Candidate Donald Trump correctly blamed the Federal Reserve for blowing up a bubble with monetary inflation and artificially low interest rates. "They're keeping the rates down so that everything else doesn't go down," said Trump as quoted in The Guardian. "We have a very false economy."[1]

Trump went on to say, ““At some point the rates are going to have to change. The only thing that is strong is the artificial stock market.”[2]

Yet not even a month after his inauguration, Trump was already on Twitter trumpeting the same stock market he had called “artificial” just a few months before:

> "Stock market hits new high with longest winning streak in decades Great level of confidence and optimism — even before tax plan rollout!"[3]

What changed? Certainly nothing that could be attributed to President Trump. The tax reform bill wouldn’t be passed until later in the year and wouldn’t take effect until 2018 (although the stock market does price future expectations). He hadn’t had time to do much on the regulatory side yet. Trump himself knew this, which is why he tried to attribute the stock markets hitting new records to confidence in his future policies.

Let’s take a look at the S&P 500 from 2001 – 2021:

Source: Wall Street Journal https://www.wsj.com/market-data/quotes/index/SPX/advanced-chart

Not even the most ardent Trump supporter honest with himself can look at this chart and conclude President Trump's policies – or any president's this century – made a significant difference in the trajectory of the S&P 500. If the years were taken away from the bottom of the chart, no one would be able to tell when President Obama left office and President Trump took over.

At the far left of the chart, the index is still falling during the aftermath of the NASDAQ meltdown and the 9/11 attacks. The Fed then cut rates to 1 percent to "stimulate" the economy, resulting in another bull run. Once it began raising rates to normalize monetary conditions, the 2008 financial crash occurred.

President Obama would have you believe it was his wise policies that revived the economy and sent the stock market on its decade-plus bull run. The reality is his inauguration was simply timed well. The market had already crashed when he was elected. It bottomed soon after he was sworn in and before any reasonable person could blame him. During his presidency, the Fed engaged in historically unprecedented monetary inflation called "quantitative easing."

The moment the Fed tried to raise interest rates slightly in December 2015,[4] there was an immediate downturn in the markets,[5] after which they ceased attempting to raise rates for another year. Of course, talking heads always attribute market selloffs to all manner of causes, but if you track the major downturns, they all line up with monetary tightening following a period of monetary inflation.

President Trump had a similar experience during his term in office. The Fed began trying to restore some semblance of normalcy beginning in December 2016 with relatively tiny increases in the Federal Funds Rate of 25 basis points per quarter. By October 2, 2018 they had reached a target rate of 2.25 percent and the market corrected by more than 10 percent.

All during this period of relatively minor tightening, President Trump publicly excoriated the Fed Chairman he appointed, Jay Powell, for doing precisely what Candidate Donald Trump said needed to be done in 2016. Suddenly, artificially low interest rates were a good thing.

Nevertheless, Powell's Fed tried one more hike to 2.5 percent in December 2018 and then very abruptly began cutting again. As a result, the "Trump boom" in the stock market resumed its course until March 2020.

It is worth noting that during the previous round of rate hikes in the mid-2000s, the Fed raised interest rates to 5.25 percent by June 2006. Rates were left there until September 2007, when it was beginning to become apparent even to the Fed that there was going to be a problem. In 2018, the markets wouldn't bear rates even half as high. This is a trend I'll cover more in a later chapter.

Just as credit isn't necessarily justified for the stock market gains during Trump's first three years in office, blaming Trump's economic policies for what happened to the markets in 2020 makes no sense, either. This was obviously the result of state governors (in concert with politicians around the world) taking the unprecedented step of shutting their economies down in response to the Covid-19 pandemic.

Whether those policies were justified or not is a subject for another book, but their economic effect was undeniable. It should be noted that the governors acted on the advice of the Trump administration's public health officials, but these were in no way economic policies that should be evaluated alongside anything that preceded them.

One result of these shock and awe policies was again unprecedented monetary inflation by the Fed in response to the crisis. Instead of merely looking at interest rate policy, it is helpful to look at the Fed's balance sheet over a period of years. This indicates the supposed value of the assets it holds based on the dollars it created to acquire them.

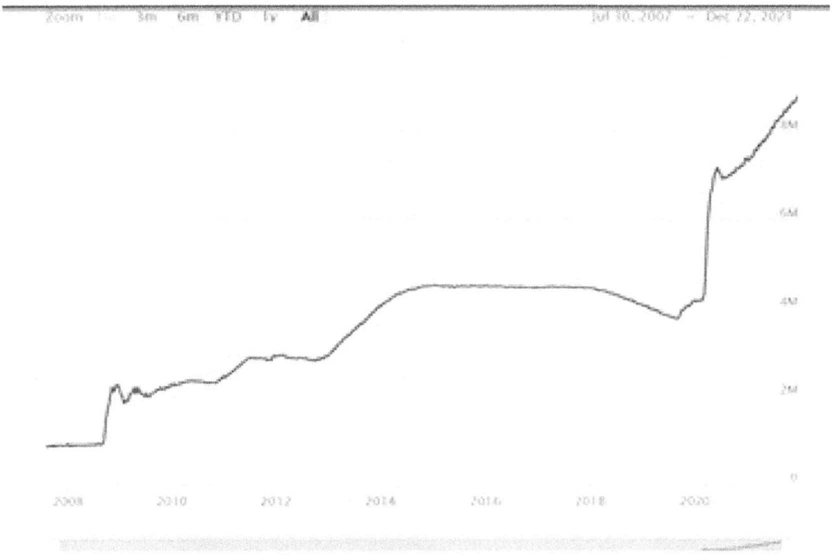

Source: Federal Reserve Official Website:

https://www.federalreserve.gov/monetarypolicy/bst_recenttrends.htm

The Federal Reserve's balance sheet included $878 billion in assets in February 2008. By September 2014 it was over $4.4 trillion, where it remained for the most part until 2018, when it began the process to "normalize" it. It didn't make it too far before the stock market reacted negatively, at which time the Fed abandoned its normalization process and began purchasing assets again.

Note that even before the staggering increase March 2020 – May 2020, the Fed had already blown its balance sheet back up over $4 trillion by early 2020, with no reason to believe that trend wouldn't have continued even without the Covid-19 interventions. So, in terms of the stock market, its performance during the Bush, Obama, Trump and Biden years can all be explained by looking at Federal Reserve monetary policy. The minor tweaks to policy made by each president pale in comparison to the sea changes in monetary policy that have occurred during this century.

What About All Those Trump Jobs?

It is common for presidents to take personal credit for "creating jobs," often quoting the number of jobs created during their administrations. They cite a highly dubious Bureau of Labor Statistics monthly nonfarm payroll report, based on a number of assumptions combined with the results of a monthly phone survey. Some economists consider the BLS jobs report meaningless, but this is the report used by presidents to justify the number of jobs they take credit for creating.

Let's take a look at the BLS nonfarm payroll numbers from 2011 – 2021. I have added a Total column to the far right of the table to annualize the monthly totals.

Year	Jan	Feb	Mar	Apr	May	Jun	Jul	Aug	Sep	Oct	Nov	Dec	Total
2011	19	212	235	314	101	236	60	126	233	204	132	202	**2074**
2012	354	262	240	82	100	73	152	172	187	159	156	239	**2176**
2013	191	278	139	191	222	181	112	242	187	225	264	69	**2301**
2014	175	166	254	325	218	326	232	188	309	252	291	268	**3004**
2015	191	271	71	284	331	174	302	125	155	306	237	273	**2720**
2016	108	212	237	197	41	258	371	143	289	118	130	214	**2318**
2017	197	183	139	220	141	211	228	190	42	249	196	179	**2175**
2018	81	378	195	153	270	214	149	229	105	212	92	240	**2318**
2019	237	-50	168	219	63	175	193	195	221	195	234	161	**2011**
2020	315	289	-1683	-20679	2833	4846	1726	1583	716	680	264	-306	**-9416**
2021	233	536	785	269	614	962	1091	483	379	546	210		**6108**

Source: Bureau of Labor Statistics Official Website

https://data.bls.gov/timeseries/CES0000000001?output_view=net_1mth

The table tells us a few things. Yes, it almost confirms President Trump's claim of having created 7 million new jobs between 2017 – 2019 (I am omitting the extraordinary job losses of 2020 for obvious reasons). The BLS shows that 6.5 million jobs were created during that period. However, the statistics also show that 8 million jobs were created during the three years prior to President Trump being inaugurated.

Does this mean President Obama did a better job of "managing the economy" than President Trump? No. A look at the totals, with all caveats about their reliability aside, show what one would expect during a business cycle caused by monetary inflation and deflation. Job creation totals increase every year from 2011 – 2014. After that, they begin to decline almost uniformly throughout Obama's last two years and Trump's first three years in office.

The one anomaly is 2018, where there is a slight increase in job creation, matching the 2016 numbers exactly, and then a decline in 2019 to the lowest total since before 2011.

Looking at the jobs numbers over the entire decade, one might conclude a cyclical bust was about to occur in early 2020 regardless of the Covid-19 pandemic and government response. Indeed, the Fed again found itself intervening in the "repo markets," which Alexander Saeedy of Fortune said at the time, "is looking a lot like it did on the precipice of the 2007 housing market crash."[6]

Record Low Unemployment

The other jobs statistic touted by presidents (when it helps them politically) is the unemployment rate. President Trump was no exception. And it is true that unemployment reached a record low during his presidency. But like so many other indicators, a little perspective is helpful. Below is a chart of the unemployment rate over the past 20 years.

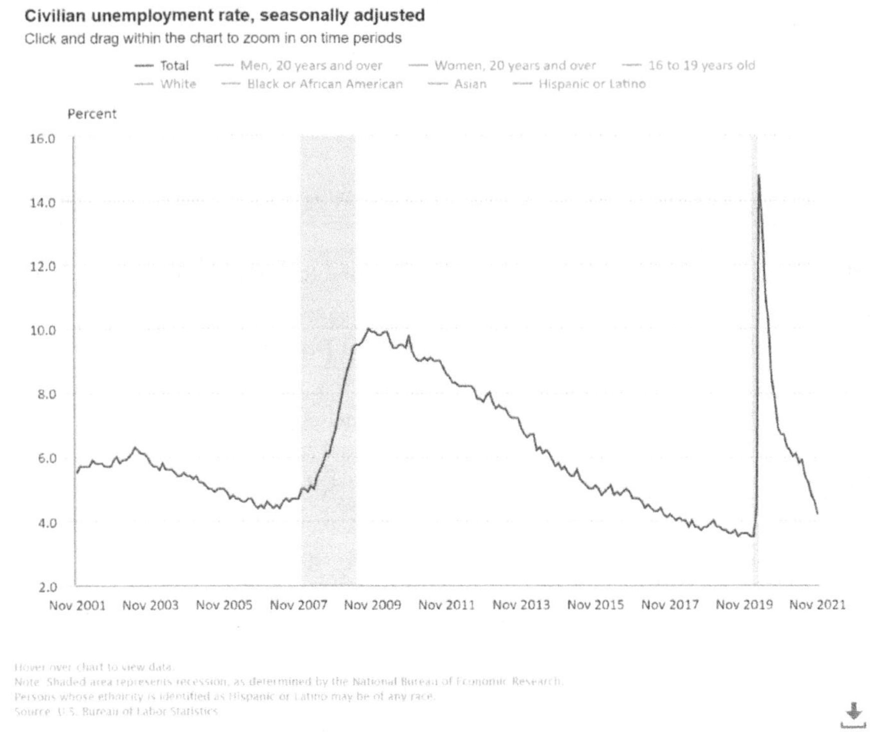

Source: Bureau of Labor Statistics Official Website

https://www.bls.gov/charts/employment-situation/civilian-unemployment-rate.htm

As with the stock market and BLS jobs reports, no honest person could look at this chart and conclude who was president at the time made any difference in the unemployment rate. Roughly coinciding with the S&P 500 chart over the same period (only in reverse), unemployment rises in the early 2000s following the NASDAQ crash and 9/11 attack. It then falls following the monetary inflation in response to that crisis until monetary deflation eventually sends it rising again, culminating in the skyrocketing unemployment following the 2008 crash.

After unemployment peaks above 10 percent in 2009, it falls steadily for the next decade. If the years were taken away, no one could point to the chart and indicate where a new president's policies took effect. Instead, we see a little uptick from 4.8% to 5.1% between January 2016 – April 2016, right after the Fed's December 2015 rate hike. Following that uptick, the unemployment rate falls slightly less rapidly until the next big crisis in March 2020.

One might be tempted to ask why job creation can ever be a bad thing. I will address that in a later chapter, along with what probably seems like the elephant in the room, namely the right side of several of the charts presented in this chapter, showing the effects of the unprecedented fiscal, economic, and monetary interventions from March 2020 to the present.

It would be unfair to conclude none of President Trump's policies were helpful. To the extent he did decrease regulation, that was likely positive. But he didn't make any sea changes to the regulatory structure in place since the New Deal.

Lowering the corporate tax rate to roughly that collected by Sweden and the other Scandinavian countries was also helpful, although it's debatable whether one is really cutting taxes if government spending goes up twice as fast as it did under one's predecessor, as it was doing under President Trump even before the 2020 crisis.[7]

Isn't that really raising taxes and simply collecting them at a different rate?

Like most presidents, Trump was a mixed bag of good and bad policies. Free market advocates liked his deregulation but not his tariffs; proponents of government intervention the opposite. But when you try to find the effects of his policies in macroeconomic indicators, they just aren't there.

CHAPTER 4

WHY AREN'T PRICES FALLING?

Originally published May 19, 2019

"When I was your age, I used to go to the movies for a dime. I'd get a big bag of candy for a nickel."

I still remember my father saying those words as I headed off to the movies in the 1970s, when the afternoon matinees cost $1.75 per ticket, more than ten times what my father had paid thirty-five years earlier. I remember because my father said that every time I went to the movies for my entire childhood and all my teenage years. I doubt I'm alone on this.

There isn't an American alive for whom steadily rising prices haven't been a fact of life for all his or her life. Most employed Americans risk their savings in the stock market, through 401Ks or other tax-deferred investments, because everyone knows merely stockpiling cash is useless. It will lose all its value because of inflation.

Just imagine if it were the other way around. Imagine if you could simply put your cash savings in the bank and without even considering any interest it would earn, see it gain value over time. Imagine if your father or grandfather repeatedly told you that something you were purchasing today used to cost him a lot *more* when he was your age.

Well, for America's first full century, that was exactly how it was (see Appendix A). Prices fluctuated year to year, but over the course of the 19th century, prices fell dramatically. A basket of goods that cost $100.00 in 1800 cost less than $50.00 in 1900. That means one could buy twice as much with the same amount of dollars. Average Americans could simply stockpile dollars over the course of their working lives and realize a return on their investment in the form of dollar appreciation.

Contrary to the absurd notion now ingrained into the minds of generations of Americans that economic growth causes inflation, that the economy can somehow, "overheat," all this price deflation occurred during the industrial revolution, a period of spectacular economic growth. That makes economic sense. As more goods and services are produced per capita and compared to the supply of dollars, the dollar prices of those goods should fall. And they did.

The 20th century was a different story. Yes, technology continued to advance, Americans continued to produce more per capita than they had previously, but prices ceased falling. That same $100 basket of goods in 1800 which had fallen to $48.94 in 1900 cost $1,265.14 in 2007. Today it costs $1,588.81. And that is using the Federal Reserve's current price inflation methodology, which is riddled with tricks to make price increases look more modest than they are.[1]

What happened? Are Americans producing far less products per capita than they did previously, as some politicians claim? Nope. Manufacturing output has steadily increased since the early 20th century, recovering from a pullback after the 2008 financial crisis to hit an all-time high earlier this year. The decrease in manufacturing jobs is mostly due to automation, not free trade deals.[2] But America produces more products than it ever has in its history.

Americans are producing so much more with so fewer people that another perennial silly idea has resurfaced – that technology will render most Americans unemployed. This idea is easily debunked,[3] but the important takeaway for our purposes here is the explosion in productivity is a massive deflationary force. It should be driving consumer goods prices down.

Also deflationary is the mass retirement of the baby boomers. Retirees only consume about 2/3 of the goods and service they previously did when they were working.[4] In other words, the wave of retirements represents a huge decrease in demand for goods and services, which should also put downward pressure on the price.

So, with these two massive deflationary forces acting upon prices, why aren't they falling? Answer: the increase in the supply of U.S. dollars has outpaced the increase of supply of goods and negated the retirees' decrease in demand. This is what the Federal Reserve has done since its inception in

1913, accelerating rapidly after 1971 and exponentially after the 2008 financial crisis.

A Federal Reserve chart of the monetary base shows the tsunami of money created by the Fed after 2008, when the monetary base was in the $800 billions. It peaked in the $4 trillions during the quantitative easing period and has only backed off to about $3.3 trillion during the modest tightening efforts since 2016. That means there is still almost four times as many U.S. dollars in existence today than there were a mere ten years ago.

Are Americans producing four times as much stuff? No, not even close. That's why prices rise every year despite all the real economic forces which should be driving them down. It's all Federal Reserve money creation – the true definition of "inflation."

During the entire progressive era, and especially since the New Deal, Americans have been taught a whole range of economic fallacies design to do one thing: keep them from realizing *they're being ripped off* every day, every hour, every minute, all for the sake of the so-called "common good."

At the root of these fallacies is the idea a currency must be "elastic" to provide "tools" for combatting depressions (now euphemistically called "recessions"). One of the tools is the central bank "adding liquidity" to the markets to create jobs. It all sounds very technical and complicated, but it's not. All quantitative easing, lowering interest rates or anything else in the Federal Reserve's so-called "toolbox" amount to is creating new money out of thin air. They can dress it up any way they want, but that's what it amounts to when all is said and done.

It's stealing. It's not as if the Fed can create new capital goods just by adding more dollars to the economy. The purchasing power must come from somewhere. Otherwise, the Fed could just produce a million dollars for everyone, and we'd all be rich. But if they aren't creating the purchasing power out of thin air, then the recipients of newly created dollars must be getting their purchasing power from someone else.

They're getting it from you. Let's say you have saved $10,000.00 in U.S. dollars. At that moment, you have the purchasing power to acquire some very small percentage of all the goods and services available at that time. Just to make the point, if there were only $1 million worth of goods and services available, you would have the purchasing power to acquire one percent of all goods and services available anywhere.

When the Fed creates new dollars and they're lent out to investors, you no longer have the purchasing power to acquire the same percentage of goods. Purchasing power has been taken from you and given to someone else, without your consent. This is "stealing," no matter how many pretty words politicians and central bankers spew to cover it up.

Americans are told this is necessary to "create jobs." But how did it become your responsibility to underwrite creating someone else's job? If it is your responsibility, why aren't you simply asked for the funds, rather than having your dollars surreptitiously depreciated?

Answer: They don't want you to realize you're being ripped off. They know that if they asked the public to give up their hard-earned savings for the sake of "creating jobs" for complete strangers, they'd never agree. So, the Fed steals your purchasing power without asking you. And, as John Maynard Keynes once said, they do it in a manner "which not one man in a million is able to diagnose."

As of this writing, the stock markets are selling off again. Media are blaming Trump's tariff tweet on Friday. That the sell-off started two days earlier is troublesome for that theory. It looks more like the market tested the Jan. 2018 high for a second time and backed away.

Trump's tariffs certainly aren't helpful and may provide a pin to burst the bubble. But when the crisis comes, it will have much less to do with Trump and much more to do with the unprecedented monetary tsunami the Fed loosed upon the world from 2008-2016.

Media are already gearing up to blame the next crash on tax cuts and deregulation, which is absurd (they're correct that government spending has something to do with it).[5]

They'll say Trump's pro-free market policies caused the crash, just as George W. Bush's supposedly did. Democratic presidential candidates will pile on that bandwagon until the axles break.

How long will the American public keep buying this story and allowing the Federal Reserve to loot them with one hand and claim to save them with the other?

CHAPTER 5

HOW THE FED STEALS FOR THE 1%

Originally published March 13, 2012

It is ironic that Occupy Wall Street is reportedly very low on cash. This is something that Wall Street itself never has to worry about. They have ready access at all times to as much cash as they need. The Occupiers mistakenly blame capitalism, but it is not capitalism that is behind this inequity. It is the completely anti-capitalist Federal Reserve System.

The Fed purports to stimulate economic growth by expanding the volume of money and credit. This forces down interest rates and makes more money available to start new businesses or expand existing ones. However, while the currency units are created out of thin air, the purchasing power is not. The purchasing power has to come from somewhere.

The expansion of money and credit really redistributes wealth from the holders of existing currency units to whoever receives the new money. When an individual "redistributes wealth" without the consent of its current owner, most people call it "stealing." Now, the Occupy movement may not have a problem with that if it results in less disparity between rich and poor. However, that's not what the Federal Reserve System is all about. The Fed steals for the 1%.

Everyone knows that the new money and credit created by the Fed flows to Wall Street. That's where big loans are made and new ventures are launched. While the borrowers do have to pay the loans back, they do so out of profits made from new capital they have acquired. The Fed silently steals this capital from everyone and transfers it to Wall Street.

This transfer is accomplished through the

phenomenon of steadily increasing prices. That is the cost of creating new money. The cost is born by the 99% while the 1% keeps all of the profits.

If the amount of currency is increased and the amount of available goods and services remain the same, prices are going to rise. You don't have to take my word for it. Sometimes a spreadsheet is worth a thousand words.

Appendix A tracks the "inflation rate" from 1800-2019. The last column (added) tracks the price movements of a basket of goods and services that cost $100.00 in 1800. As you can see, prices dropped dramatically over time throughout the 19th century. That same basket of goods that cost $100.00 in 1800 cost only $56.74 in 1912.

It is important to understand the implications of this phenomenon for 19th century workers. It made them richer. Someone making $200.00 per year in 1912 was twice as wealthy as someone making $200.00 per year in 1800. While wages increased less in the 19th century than in the 20th, purchasing power for the average worker rose dramatically. This is the natural result of society becoming more productive. As the supply of goods goes up, all things being equal, the price of goods goes down.

Contrary to Ben Bernanke's warnings of the horrors of "deflation," falling prices were the norm throughout the period in American history when the economy and the middle class expanded most dramatically. Yes, great fortunes were made by a few, but they had to be made honestly when money was honest. Most importantly, the common worker became wealthier during this period. He didn't have to risk his savings in the stock market just to keep up with inflation. He could simply save cash and watch his purchasing power increase over time, instead of vanish.

Now, look at the same basket of goods from 1913 (the year the Fed was created) through 2008. You see exactly the opposite trend. The same basket of goods that cost $56.74 in 1912 now costs $1,265.14. Obviously, even the more dramatic increase in wages during this period has not kept up with the increase in prices. This makes the average worker poorer.

The Fed is the reason that average Americans have worked harder and become more productive over the past century yet have not experienced a corresponding increase in wealth. It is why two people in the average family have to hold jobs just to provide the lifestyle formerly provided by one. The Fed is behind the widening gap between rich and poor.

People from different ends of the political spectrum will never agree on everything. However, they can work together on those things that they do agree on, such as stopping a war or abolishing bad laws. If the Occupiers turn their attention to the Federal Reserve System, they will be surprised at the people they will find standing by their side. Libertarians, independents, and even a Republican presidential candidate will join them on this. Let's get rid of *99% of the problem now* and argue about the other 1% later. Occupy the Fed.

CHAPTER 6

MICHAEL MOORE WANTS TO END THE FED (HE JUST DOESN'T KNOW IT YET)

Originally published October 4, 2009

"You keep on using that word. I do not think it means what you think it means."

- Mandy Patinkin as Inigo Montoya in *The Princess Bride* (1987)

It is ironic that Michael Moore's latest movie, *Capitalism: A Love Story* features two appearances by writer and comedic actor Wallace Shawn. There is even a clip of Shawn exclaiming "Inconceivable!" in his hilarious turn as Vezzini in *The Princess Bride.* However, the most appropriate clip from that movie would have been Inigo Montoya uttering the words quoted in the prologue of this article. Using one of Moore's staple filmmaking techniques, he could have cut to the clip immediately after one of his own pronouncements about capitalism. For although Moore says the word over and over throughout the movie, it is apparent that it "doesn't mean what he thinks it means."

The closest thing to a definition of capitalism that Moore provides to his audience comes early on when he remarks, "Capitalism: a system of giving and taking – mostly taking." He goes on to show a half dozen or so clips of people extolling capitalism for providing "the freedom to succeed and to fail" or hailing the virtues of competition. However, the common mistake made by both Moore when attacking capitalism and the Republican politicians he depicts defending it is their mutual failure to recognize the central tenet of capitalism: property rights.

True capitalism is based upon one simple principle: that all exchanges of property are made with the voluntary consent of all parties. Private ownership of property and competition – the other two components of capitalism in most traditional definitions – are actually results of this foundational principle. As all governments are institutions of coercion, there is no way for them to acquire property through voluntary exchange. Further, with all exchanges being voluntary, sellers must by definition compete with one another in order to sell their products. So, the foundation of "capitalism" is really the non-aggression principle applied to property. Capitalism requires that no one's property can be taken from them without their consent.

However, Moore's film does not examine anything close to that system, which Adam Smith called "a system of natural liberty" (the word "capitalism" was not coined until nearly a century later). There is a good reason for that – it doesn't exist. What Moore mistakes for capitalism is really the soft fascism that has been increasing in intensity in the United States since the Federal Reserve and income tax were created and property rights were destroyed. He makes the same mistake that Republican voters make when they vote Republican politicians into office. They believe the politicians when they say that they support "free markets," despite the fact that they go on to govern in exactly the opposite way.

The injustices that Moore depicts in his film are without exception caused by government. Not one can be traced to people voluntarily exchanging their goods and services with one another. What Moore represents as "capitalism" is really what Thomas Dilorenzo described as "Hamilton's Curse" in his 2008 book of the same name. Without attempting to reduce Dilorenzo's treatise to a few sentences, he generally describes the economic system whereby the government allies itself with the wealthiest segment of society in order to plunder the wealth of everyone else in pursuit of "national greatness" or "the common good." The hallmarks of the system are corporate welfare, deficit spending by government, protectionist tariffs, and most importantly, a central bank with a government-granted monopoly on the creation of money.

This system purports to benefit society by encouraging the growth of domestic industry and thereby increasing the power and standing of the nation as a whole, as well as providing employment for the working class. However, like socialism, it must achieve "societal goals" by violating the fundamental principle of capitalism. It must violate the non-aggression principle by taking property away from people without their consent and redistributing that property to others. Some of this is accomplished through taxation. A much greater part is accomplished through monetary inflation.

It is astounding that most people are able to ignore the fact that the central bank is an instrument of theft and thereby completely antagonistic to capitalism. It takes an incredible dearth of healthy skepticism not to question the reason for legal tender laws, which force people to use the central bank's currency. There is only one reason for these laws: without them no one would choose to accept an un-backed paper currency in exchange for their real goods or services. People are forced to use Federal Reserve Notes so that the government and its corporate allies can use inflation (expansion of the money supply) to transfer wealth from everyone in society to the privileged few who benefit from the transfer. The beneficiaries include corporate defense contractors, large farming corporations, Wall Street banks, and other "pillars of the economy." It is inflation more than anything else that widens the gap between rich and poor. It is the chief vehicle for what Bastiat described as "the few plunder the many."

However, Michael Moore does not recognize the right to the fruits of one's labor and so he is completely blind to the difference between capitalism and the system promoted by Republican politicians (in deed if not in word). He fails to see that every aspect of our financial meltdown was caused by some violation of property rights, representing a departure from capitalism.

The money needed to extend all of those "deceptive mortgages" was created by the Federal Reserve out of thin air, thus diluting the value of all existing U.S. dollars. This was a theft from the holders of those existing dollars. Most of the loans themselves were guaranteed by Fannie and Freddie Mac, which uses the coercive power of government to use taxpayer money as collateral for people who would either not receive those loans or who would pay a much higher interest rate. Again, this is not capitalist voluntary exchange but instead wealth redistribution and a distortion of the free market. Similarly, the hundreds of billions paid out to defense contractors and other beneficiaries of President Bush's wars in the Middle East were also funded by inflation, which the Republicans overtly flaunted by cutting taxes while skyrocketing government spending.

Since he fails to recognize that it was violation of property rights that truly caused our economic meltdown, he doesn't recommend the restoration of property rights as the solution. Moore blindly accepts the traditional "progressive" fallacy that free market participants can only benefit at someone else's expense, instead of recognizing that people who exchange voluntarily do so to their mutual benefit. As a result, he accepts government's role as plunderer of property and merely suggests dividing up the loot differently. He promotes the bogus idea that the government can grant rights to people, and suggests that the coercive power of government no longer be used to redistribute to the wealthy, but instead be used to redistribute to everyone else. He objects to a system wherein the few plunder the many, but suggests it be replaced with a system where "everybody plunders everybody."

Moore asserts that FDR had the answer when he proposed a "Second Bill of Rights," granting Americans the right to a reasonable wage, health care, a pension, and other entitlements. Again, as the concept of property rights is foreign to him, Moore is able to ignore the fact that granting a right to these things means that those who provide them have no rights. He extols the "justice" of labor unions, but ignores the fact that it was the unions that destroyed the U.S. automakers by claiming exactly these rights. It was actually an alliance between government and these unions – identical in principle to the alliance between government and Wall Street - that turned his beloved Flint into a ghost town. He suggests that we should set these forces loose upon all of society. His ability to ignore reality is, to quote Mr. Shawn, "inconceivable."

Like all of his movies, *Capitalism: A Love Story* is very well made. Moore is exceptionally good at what he does, bringing wit, comedic timing, and emotional power to the screen. Also like all of his movies, he identifies real injustices and expresses appropriate outrage at them. However, throughout his distinguished career he has made the classic mistake of misidentifying the cause of the problems he depicts so poignantly on the screen.

He compares the United States to Rome and points to the similarities between our problems and theirs. He correctly identifies half of the cause of Rome's decline and ours: the government's unholy alliance with a landed aristocracy that plunders the wealth of the people for redistribution to the privileged few. However, he fails to recognize his solution as the other half of the cause of both Rome's decline and ours: the rest of society attempting to share in the plunder by means of majority vote (democracy). It was both of these forces acting together which destroyed Rome's currency and led to her eventual collapse. Like Rome, we are also afflicted with both of these ills.

The only real solution to our predicament is to implement a system that supports Bastiat's third alternative – "where nobody plunders anybody." It is only by following this principle that justice can truly prevail. The most significant step in achieving such a system would be to eliminate the Federal Reserve System. Neither the Republican system of plunder for the wealthy nor the Democratic system of plunder for everybody is possible without monetary inflation. There is no way that government could ever achieve either through direct taxation.

I believe that Michael Moore's intentions are good. At the end of his film, he asks Americans to join him. I have an alternative proposition for him. If he truly wants to see justice restored in America, along with equal opportunity for all Americans to pursue their happiness, he should call off his misguided attack on capitalism and *join us* to End the Fed.

CHAPTER 7

OWS AND THE TEA PARTY: IN THE BALLPARK BUT HAVEN'T FOUND THEIR SEATS

Originally published November 7, 2011

As the 2012 elections approach, there is now a left-wing protest movement to mirror the right-wing Tea Party. Occupy Wall Street (OWS) and its many offshoots claims to represent "the 99%" of Americans who are not among the richest 1%. Like the Tea Party, OWS sees economic catastrophe ahead if America's economic system is not fundamentally changed. However, unlike the Tea Party, which places the blame for America's economic woes on the doorstep of politicians, OWS points the finger squarely at Wall Street - and anyone else that makes enough money to qualify for a "1%" membership card.

It is actually refreshing to see Americans from both sides of the political spectrum interested enough to actually object to *something*. Whether marching around and carrying signs actually accomplishes anything is debatable. However, the Tea Party has already shown that political careers can be made or ended when enough people get both fed up and organized. While OWS is not as politically organized as the Tea Party was at this point in 2009, it has already made it over the toughest hurdle - getting a critical mass of people off the couch and out into the streets. As labor unions and other left wing special interests get more involved, it is likely that a bona fide political movement will emerge from the present confusion. Like the Tea Party, OWS might even change a few seats on their side of the aisle. But what then?

If the results of the Tea Party Congress are any indication, the answer to that question is "nothing." Yes, the new Congress made some symbolic statements, like requiring the members to read the Constitution aloud during the opening session. However, when it came to actually advancing their supposed agenda in a substantive way - cutting the size of the federal government and reigning in deficits - not much happened. A proposal emerged to cut $100 billion out of the $1.6 trillion deficit, which would have been meaningless even if it passed. Beyond that, it's been business as usual inside the Capitol, with Congressmen from both sides of the aisle continuing to spend money that the federal government doesn't have and kicking the can a little further down the road.

Left wing Americans should already know that the electoral process is unlikely to produce substantive change. As the third year of Obama's presidency draws to a close, there is almost nothing of substance that either his supporters or his critics can point to that differentiates his presidency from that of George W. Bush. Both championed and got passed an expansion of government involvement in the health care system that costs taxpayers about $100 billion per year directly and likely causes distoritions in the health care market that are far more costly than that. Both started a few new wars in the Middle East. Both expanded the federal government's power to spy on its own citizens. Both passed "sweeping regulatory reforms" that further crippled America's already weak economy. Both expanded executive power unconstitutionally. Both set new precedents in attacking the Bill of Rights.

However, the similarity between the two that should resonate most with OWS supporters is this one: both filled their cabinets with Wall Street and corporate insiders and never made a move that those special interests didn't like. Sure, Obama made some populist, anti-business statements early in his presidency, but when it came to "Change" in the healthcare system, his program turned out to be a half trillion pear year handout to the health insurance industry. That wasn't exactly what the true believers had in mind, but it was business as usual for corporate-owned Washington.

In short, two hugely trumpeted "revolutions" in American politics - a leftwing one in 2008 and a right-wing one in 2010 - have failed to move the needle one degree in Washinton, D.C. A lot of articles were written and a lot of television talk shows were provided with material about both, but absolutely nothing has changed. Sooner or later, one has to answer the question: Why not?

The answer is that even the genuine grassroots members from both the left and the right don't understand what is ailing America. They know something is wrong, but decades of government propaganda bolstered by shoddy education have left most Americans unequipped to figureout what it is. In fact, both the Tea Party and OWS share the same fundamental misconceptions about The Problem.

Both the Tea Party and OWS believe that Republican presidents, especially Ronald Reagan, had somehow created a laissez faire capitalist economy during their presidencies. The Tea Partiers believe that America must get back to Reaganomics, while OWS believes it was the root cause of today's problems. Both of them are wrong. Neither Ronald Reagan nor George W. Bush signed one bill that substantively made the American economy more laissez faire. In fact, Bush actually signed Sarbanes-Oxley, which he himself called "the most sweeping regulatory reform since the New Deal." Even what the media called "deregulation" during the Reagan years was mostly regulatory tweaks that were passed under Carter. In short, "deregulation" never happened. It was just one huge, Jedi mind trick, similar to "hope and change."

That brings us to misconception number two: regulation itself. Both movements misunderstand the relationship between our present corporate economy and government regulation. The Tea Party believes that getting rid of regulations as Reagan supposedly did would "get the government out of the way" of America's corporations, resulting in huge gains in productivity and employment. OWS believes that more regulations will reign in "corporate greed" and protect the little guy from those same rapacious corporations. Again, both of them are wrong.

A truly unregulated free market would not result in a few, large corporations controlling every economic sector. Nor would it result in most of society's wealth being concentrated within a small percentage of the population. While no one alive has ever lived under such a system in terms of the entire economy, we have seen it in a particular sector within the last two decades. As Bill Bonner pointed out, the high tech industry existed for a time as an unregulated free market. Did this result in entrenched corporations getting bigger and concentrating even more wealth in the hands of a few? Absolutely not. Bonner reminds us, "They created an entirely new industry...with new companies nobody had ever heard of. And then, they destroyed some of the biggest businesses in America."[1]

Government regulation creates barriers to entry for new firms and dampens innovation. In other words, it insulates entrenched corporations from competition, causing the very consolidation and concentration of wealth that OWS objects to. That's why established corporations never object to new regulations. Why should they? They end up writing the regulations themselves with one thing in mind - protect their position from the competition that would occur in a free market. That's what makes left wing support for increased government regulation so tragically ironic. It's like they are rushing to the scene of a fire with a sistern full of gasoline.

The Tea Party purports to favor less government regulation, but they have no idea what the results would be. They, too, do not understand the difference between our present corporatist system and a free market. Were the economy truly deregulated, most of the corporate giants that they hold up as symbolic of the free market would be gone. Only those that could deliver better products at lower prices in the face of unrelenting competition would survive - and only for as long as they could continue to do so. Upward mobility would return. Large fortunes would again be made by "college drop-outs, computer nerds, products of teenage mothers and broken marriages" (Bonner again), just as the misnamed "robber barons" largely came from the ranks of the poor. Conservatives didn't like that in the 19th century - and they might not like it now, either. But that's what the free market does. It rewards innovation, productivity, and achievement, regardless of the social pedigree of the innovator.

Neither OWS nor the Tea Party recognizes how economically destructive the gargantuan U.S. military establishment is. There were some left wing protests against the Iraq War during the Bush years, but that is a non-issue for OWS. Now that there is a Democrat running the empire, the left seems to have made its peace with war. The left never objected to the continuation of the decades-long occupations of Europe, Japan, Korea, or the 130 or so other countries that the U.S. government currently has troops in. In purely economic terms, those programs dwarf the active wars.

Of course, support for this trillion-dollar-a-year abomination is a key plank of the Tea Party movement, which is against taking money from one American and using it to buy healthcare for another American, but has no problem taking money from one American and using to (supposedly) buy "freedom" for people in other countries. Not only is this direct transfer of wealth draining America of scarce resources, but it has completely skewed what's left of American manufacturing towards producing products that don't increase wealth. Wealth is only increased when products are produced that people *voluntarily* buy. No one voluntarily buys weapons or the services of military personnel. And those resources in turn don't produce anything at all.

Both the left and the right view imperialism as somehow part and parcel of laissez faire capitalism. Nothing could be further from the truth. The foundation of capitalism is voluntary exchange. There is nothing that a military force can do under the guise of "protecting America's vital interests" or "opening up markets for American companies" that has anything to do with capitalism or voluntary exchange. Even if an army really did influence people in other countries to trade with American companies, that would not be capitalism any more than Fannie Mae or Freddie Mac influencing people to take out loans was capitalism. When it's not voluntary, it's not a free market. Whatever it's true purpose is(and there are a lot of theories about that), the U.S. government's massive military establishment is just another large, bankrupt government program.

However, the most harmful misconception that OWS and the Tea Party share is not really a misconception at all. It is the failure to recognize the most destructive element in the American economy - the Federal Reserve. The failure of either movement to make the Federal Reserve a priority or even acknowledge its existence explains many of the other misconceptions. Both the artificial booms that each attribute to their presidents of choice - Clinton for liberals, Reagan for conservatives- and the inevitable busts that each blame on presidents of the other party- Carter and Obama for conservatives, Bush 1 and Bush 2 for liberals - can all be traced back to the predictable results of Federal Reserve monetary policy. Even if all of the other economic interventions were eliminated and this one intervention were left in place, most of the economic problem would still exist.

The Tea Party claims to oppose Obama's "socialism," but fails to see the Federal Reserve as a fundamentally socialist institution. Its stated purpose is to transfer wealth from one individual or group to another at the direction of central economic planners. It doesn't get much more socialist than that. A few conservatives might object to the way that a particular Fed chairman conducts the business of the Fed, but almost none object to the Fed itself. Yet compared to the transfer of wealth that occurs when the Fed inflates the currency, all of the U.S. government's welfare programs combined pale in comparison. Since the Fed transfers wealth to Wall Street and corporate America, one might understand their reluctance to oppose that aspect of it. But what about a small group of government hacks attempting to direct the entire economy? If that's not "socialism," then what is?

OWS is similarly disinterested in the Federal Reserve, even though it exists to transfer wealth from the 99% to the 1%. For both groups, ignorance is probably the majority of the problem. The Fed has managed to stay out of the spotlight for most of the past century, taking the credit for supposed recoveries and avoiding all blame for the business cycle itself. Yet, even if it did what it purported to do, it should still be Public Enemy No. 1 to both OWS and the Tea Party. Until most Americans understand how destructive this institution is, no amount of "reform" is going to make our economic problems go away.

So, the next election will be influenced by two grassroots movements committed to solving America's problems. One says that the problem is government. They are right. The other says it is corporations and the financial elite. They are also right. As a friend of mine likes to say, both groups "are in the ball park, but they haven't found their seat." One can only hope for a moment of clarity on both sides. If they could only see things as they really are, they'd be marching side by side.

CHAPTER 8

CENTRAL BANKING DOESN'T WORK

JUST ASK THE FED

Originally published January 26, 2010

Hopefully, the question of whether there should be a Federal Reserve will be on the table someday. In the meantime, there is another question to ask: Can it do what it purports to do?

According to the Federal Reserve's website, its mission is as follows:

Today, the Federal Reserve's duties fall into four general areas:

• conducting the nation's monetary policy by influencing the monetary and credit conditions in the economy in pursuit of maximum employment, stable prices, and moderate long-term interest rates

• supervising and regulating banking institutions to ensure the safety and soundness of the nation's banking and financial system and to protect the credit rights of consumers

• maintaining the stability of the financial system and containing systemic risk that may arise in financial markets

• providing financial services to depository institutions, the U.S. government, and foreign official institutions, including playing a major role in operating the nation's payments system[1]

Of these four stated goals, the first is the most expansive in its scope. Let us leave it until last. The second, to ensure the soundness of the banking system, seems to have been answered by history. Since the Fed's launch in 1914, the nation has suffered banking crises in every generation that have dwarfed the Panic of 1907 or any of its predecessors. In addressing the Great Depression, the Savings and Loan Crisis, and the 2008 Meltdown, the Federal Reserve's only answer has been, "Without the Fed, it would have been much worse." History is not on the Fed's side. Only ignorance of the facts allows the Fed to keep fooling most of the people most of the time.

Refuting the third stated goal is so easy it's almost embarrassing. For those not trying to regain their seats after falling on the floor laughing, I need only to point out 30-1 leveraging, $60 trillion (or more?) in derivatives [2], or the subprime mortgage disaster. I believe that to go any farther would be, to borrow a football analogy, "piling on".

In fact, Alan Greesnpan's now famous (or infamous) mea culpa on the "flaw" in his beliefs about the self-regulating nature of financial markets effectively amounts to the Fed admitting that it has failed in goals three and four. If the "Maestro" himself doesn't speak for the Federal Reserve, then who does?

Regarding that fourth goal, one is tempted to give this one to the Fed. The important objection would be of the "should they" rather than of the "can they" variety. The fact that the Fed provides these services with an exclusive monopoly and claims only that it will play a “major role," rather than a positive one, makes this the least significant of the four.

That leaves the first goal, which is stable prices, full employment, and moderate long term interest rates. There can be no doubt that the promises of stable prices and full employment in particular are now the principle justifications for the existence of the Federal Reserve. Almost exclusively, when the subject of the Fed comes up, these two goals are discussed. Even the Fed chairmen themselves, when testifying before Congress, often state these two goals exclusively in describing the Fed's overall mission.

It should not be forgotten that until the late 1970's, full employment was not part of the Fed's mandate. Even using the logic of central banking proponents, these two goals are mutually exclusive of one another. Since the only means the Fed has at its disposal to try to achieve full employment is expansion of the supply of money and credit, which puts upward pressure on prices, the Fed must balance these two goals to try to find the optimum level of money and credit where everyone is employed but prices remain stable.

Ironically, the best source of information on the Fed's performance in terms of its principle goal for the first sixty years of its existence (price stability) is the Fed itself. Among the collections of historical data on the Federal Reserve of Minneapolis website, there can be found a table documenting price inflation rates for every year since 1800 (Appendix A of this article). There, one can see for oneself whether or not the Fed provided price stability during any period in its existence.

The first fact that jumps off of the page is the stark difference in the trends before and after the creation of the Fed. For the period from 1800-1913, the general price level (a statistic that Austrian economists object to) was cut almost in half. In other words, products that on average cost $100.00 in 1800 would only cost $58.10 in 1913. While there were some years where prices rose, prices generally fell overall during the entire 19th century.

This would probably be a startling revelation to most modern Americans. There isn't an American alive whose parents or grandparents haven't remarked at current price levels and gone on to say, "When I was your age, I only paid a dime for that." As unbelievable as it might seem, that conversation would have been exactly the opposite in 1890. Grandpa would instead be saying, "When I was your age, I had to pay a lot more for that." Today, Americans resign themselves to constantly rising prices as a fact of life. However, that is a phenomenon that has only occurred since the creation of the Fed.

In contrast to the century preceding the Fed, the century following has seen exactly the opposite result. Those same products whose average price had fallen from $100.00

in 1800 to $58.10 in 1913 rose to $1,265.14 in 2008. That is an increase of over 2,000%!

Without addressing the subject of which result is "better for society," inflation or deflation, the data speak directly to the question of "price stability." From 1800-1913, the average annual fluctuation in price was 3.4%. From 1914-2008, the average annual fluctuation in price was 4.5%, a *33% increase over the previous period.* In fact, the numbers for the Fed would be far worse if the same methods used to calculate the price inflation rate were used for the entire period from 1914-2008. In the 1990's, several changes were made to the methodology used to calculate the Consumer Price Index. They all have the effect of lowering the price inflation rate given a particular set of price data.

Regarding the goal of "full employment," the Fed's results are also poor. Similar to that of the CPI, the methodology for calculating the unemployment rate was also changed in the 1990's. These changes in methodology, which include no longer counting "discouraged workers," lower the unemployment rate from what it would be for the same data if calculated using the old methodology.

Despite this handicap, the Fed still fails to achieve positive results. The average annual unemployment rate in the U.S. between 1948 and 1978 was 5.1% (see Appendix B). Even without compensating for the changes in methodology during the 1990's, the average annual unemployment rate in the U.S. between 1979 and 2009 was 6.1%. So, unemployment was almost 20% higher during the period that the Fed actively tried to manage it than it was during the prior 30 years.

Once you undo the methodological changes in calculating price inflation and unemployment that were put in place in the 1990's, the Fed's results on price stability and unemployment get much uglier. Nevertheless, even after the Fed fudges its own numbers it still comes out a failure. Everyone can remember the ne'er-do-well from school that cheated on tests and still couldn't pass. Would we want that kid managing the entire economy?

The arguments the Fed makes to justify its existence are fraught with false assumptions. One is that "stable prices" are a good thing. Remember, the industrial revolution occurred amidst steadily falling prices. It was this period of steady price deflation (gasp!) that saw the common people become the prime market for society's output - for the first time in human history. It was this period that saw the United States transform itself in a matter of decades from an indebted hodgepodge of former colonies to a world economic power. The natural result of economic progress and increased productivity is falling prices. That is what raises the standard of living for the majority of society.

However, the most absurd assumption underlying the arguments for the Fed is one common to all collectivist arguments: that there is some strange entity called "society" whose needs outweigh the rights of every individual that comprises it. Every citizen surrenders his right to liberty to legal tender laws because being forced to use the Fed's fraudulent notes as currency supposedly benefits "society."

He surrenders his right to property in letting the Fed steal his savings silently through inflation for the same reason. In the end, however, the Fed fails to achieve its "societal" goals of full employment and stable prices, so he gives up his rights for nothing. Isn't time he took them back? There is a way: End the Fed.

Chapter 9

THE CATALYST NOT THE CAUSE

Originally published June 23, 2008

There is an inherent contradiction between free markets that reward productive achievement with honestly earned wealth and a central planning apparatus that arbitrarily controls the real cost of investment, how much investment there will be, and ultimately what the fruits of your labor will be worth. In a country that proclaims itself to be the "land of the free," central banking doesn't sound good, it doesn't feel good, and, most importantly, it doesn't work. However, the Federal Reserve System is merely the catalyst of malinvestment and economic cycles. If we really want solve the problems of economic cycles and invisible wealth transfer, we have to eliminate the root cause: fractional reserve banking.

Andrew Jackson is often cited as a hero for killing the Second Bank of the United States. While this did indeed put a limit on money creation and credit expansion, it is easy to forget who paid the price for those limits: depositors. During the "free banking" period from 1837-1862, the average lifespan of a bank was about 5 years, and roughly half of the banks failed, largely due to their inability to honor deposits. Bank failures contracted the money supply, keeping the value of money relatively stable.

That was great if you had a safe full of gold coins. However, if your life savings was stored in a failed bank, you lost it all. When a bank failed, everyone that did not withdraw their deposited money lost their deposits. Both the wealthy financier and the retiree of modest means were harmed.

Fractional reserve banking allows the bank to lend out money on deposit while keeping the deposited money simultaneously available to the depositor. Thus, the money it actually has is merely "a fraction" of the total deposits. This certainly provides a huge opportunity to the bank, which can make astronomical profits. It also allows depositor to earn interest on a savings account. It can accelerate economic growth, by providing loans for business investment beyond the real savings rate for a particular economy.

However, the downside of fractional reserve banking is one we are all familiar with. With liquidity in the system equaling as much as 10 times the real savings on deposit, negative consequences are virtually inevitable. First, prices are going to go up. Fiat money retains its value based upon its scarcity. Ron Paul uses an excellent metaphor in his book, *The Revolution: A Manifesto*, when he asks the rhetorical question, "Or imagine an art auction in which the bidders are given an additional million dollars. Would we not expect bids to go up?"[1]

Second, malinvestment is going to occur. A scarcity of money and credit forces lenders to use higher standards when deciding whether or not to make a loan. They will always lend out to what they believe are the investments that have the best combination of risk and return. The natural tendency for a lender is to limit his risk, while seeking those investments where the return is the highest and most certain.

However, as the money supply is increased and there is still money available *after* the most optimal investments have been made, the remaining money gets invested in ventures that have more risk, or less certain expectation of return, or both. Loans are granted to people or companies that would not have received them without the additional "liquidity" available to lenders. When the money supply is inflated hundreds of billions or even trillions of dollars beyond real savings, you get a bubble.

A bubble is a critical mass of malinvestment that causes whole sectors of the economy to become overvalued. Of course, once it becomes obvious that those investments are never going to yield a return, the bubble pops, and a recession follows. During the recession, all of those malinvestments are liquidated, debts are paid down, and general contraction in the economy occurs. This is usually accompanied by higher unemployment.

Throughout history, the practice of fractional reserve banking and the inevitable bank failures that accompany it have motivated calls for a lender of last resort, or a central bank.[1] If you are going to allow fractional reserve banking, you must either resign yourself that bank failures are going to be common from time to time, and that there is no "guaranteed" place to store and safeguard your savings, or that a central bank is necessary to create out of thin air the money needed when banks cannot honor all of their withdrawal requests.

Thus, the central bank perpetuates fractional reserve banking when it would otherwise fail. Moreover, by intervening in the free market by artificially setting interests rates, the central bank actually promotes faster and greater

---

[1] De Soto, Jesus Huerta *Money, Banking, and Economic Cycles* (English Edition) Ludwig Von Mises Institute Auburn, Alabama 2006 pg. 713

expansion of the money supply. If fractional reserve banking were a chemical reaction, the central bank would be the catalyst, accelerating the process with its infusions of "liquidity" through interest rate manipulation and open market operations.

In order for real economic growth to occur, savers must consume less than they produce. The resulting savings provide capital for growth. The saver must then trade consumption today for a return on investment tomorrow. In the terms of the economist, he must trade present goods for future goods.

Fractional reserve banking attempts to do away with this reality. It tells the saver that he does not have to sacrifice present goods at all but can still expect future goods. When you open a savings account that pays interest, you and your banker pretend that your banker can not only safeguard your money for you for free, but can actually pay you for the privilege and still stay in business. He cannot. The only way that he can pay you interest on that deposited money is by investing your money somewhere else.

Fractional reserve banking is really a kind of insanity, where you give money to your banker, he lends it out, and you both pretend it is still sitting in the vault at your disposal. It violates a universal law that most 8-year-olds know but most bankers have forgotten: You can't have your cake and eat it, too.

In order to fully understand these issues, one must understand the nature of money. What is money? It is a store of value and a medium of exchange. It is a practical way for people producing a wide variety of different goods and services to trade those goods and services with each other. It allows the grower of apples to trade with the manufacturer of automobiles without requiring the manufacturer to accept 20,000 apples at once for his automobile.

Economists usually divide money into three categories. The first is commodity money. Commodity money is unique in that it has some non-monetary value. While gold is often the example used, I believe grain is a better one to understand this concept.

At certain times and places in history, grain has been used as money. It is relatively uniform, easily divisible, somewhat imperishable, and scarce enough that it can function as money. When the automobile manufacturer trades his product for grain, he can store it for years without it spoiling. He can divide it into bushels, one-pound sacks, cups, or even tablespoons, allowing him to buy goods and services of varying value. He can use it to trade for furniture for his house, or meat, or his electric service.

If all else fails, and there are not sellers available to provide him something he wants in exchange for his grain, he can eat it. Gold and silver are other common examples of commodity money.

Storing the necessary amount of grain to meet all of the needs for money in a modern society is of course inconvenient and carrying enough grain on your person even to get through the day would be even more so. That is what gives rise to a second type of money, representative money. The U.S. dollar, when it was redeemable for a fixed amount of gold, was representative money. The defining characteristic of representative money is that, while it has no non-monetary value of its own, it is directly redeemable for commodity money or a hard asset. This makes its value relatively stable, because you can always redeem it for grain, gold, or whatever hard asset the representative money is exchangeable for.

The U.S. dollar today fits into a third category of money, fiat money. Fiat money neither has non-monetary value itself nor is it redeemable for a hard asset or commodity money. Its legitimacy is "bestowed upon it by fiat," and its value ultimately depends solely upon the confidence of those using it that it will be accepted in exchange for goods and services the holder will want.

While there is a tendency today to associate inflation and the business cycle completely with fiat money and the Federal Reserve System, the bank failures of the free banking period all occurred while the U.S. was without a central bank and still on the gold standard. Is the only answer for us to carry around bushels full of grain?

No. What is really needed is a 100% reserve ratio.

This means that banks are only allowed to loan out money that is made available to them for that purpose by customers. Banks would not be able to loan out deposited money that is simultaneously available to the depositor.

There is a cost to this proposition that most people will find pretty easy to live with. Savings accounts would no longer pay interest. In fact, bankers would be due a reasonable fee for safekeeping the depositor's money without exposing it to any risk. A bank customer who wished to earn interest on his money would have to agree to loan the money to the bank for an agreed upon term, during which the money would not be available to the depositor. We make these loans now; they are called Certificates of Deposit (CD's). There is also a degree of risk in this, in that the bank could make bad loans. However, history shows that banks are pretty good at evaluating risk when not flooded with cheap, fiat currency.

Wall Street would pay a higher price in that growth and investment would be slower, although much steadier and less likely to be imaginary. Many billionaires would have to resign themselves to being millionaires. However, they would be comforted by the knowledge that they had earned those millions, instead of having indirectly stolen billions from the poor and middle class through inflation.

Perhaps a private charity could be founded to help those millionaires having trouble making ends meet.

In return for these sacrifices (if you can call them that), economic growth would be real. No longer would there be inflationary bubbles, like the 1990's tech bubble or this decade's real estate bubble, or the painful recessions that follow them. With every investment relying on real savings rather than fiat "liquidity," standards would be much higher and malinvestment would be significantly reduced. While malinvestment and business cycles could still occur, they would be infinitesimally milder than the booms and busts we experience now. We would no longer need a Federal Reserve to bail out banks during a run. In fact, a run on the bank would be of little consequence since the bank would have 100% of the depositors' money available.

Moreover, without over-expansion of the money

supply, the wealth transfer from the poor and middle class to the wealthy would cease. We would have less billionaires, but we would have a higher standard of living for most people. The gap between rich and poor would begin to close, with most people landing very comfortably in the middle. The quality of life for the poor would again begin to improve, as it improved during the nineteenth century.

Our steps might take a little longer, but we would no longer take a step back after every two steps forward. After thousands of years of invisible wealth transfer, bankers would no longer inherit the earth. All of this is possible but reinstituting a gold standard and abolishing the Federal Reserve would not be enough. We must finally end the insane practice of fractional reserve banking.

CHAPTER 10

FOLLOW THE SCIENCE?

Originally published February 27, 2011

On February 9th, Rep. Ron Paul of Texas chaired his first meeting of the House Monetary Policy Subcommittee that he now leads due to the Republican victories in last November's congressional elections. Congressman Paul invited several expert witnesses to testify to the committee on their opinions about monetary policy. Among these were Austrian economist Tom Dilorenzo.

Much has been made of Rep. Lacy Clay's attack on Dilorenzo's credibility due to his alleged association with a "politically incorrect" group called the League of the South. However, Clay also attacked the Austrian school of economics itself, calling the "Austrian deductive method a non-rigorous scientific method." Clay bases this allegation on the fact that Austrian theory is not based upon "an empirical method to study economics." He refers to the fact that the Austrian school does not recognize the Keynesian theoretical models or the aggregate data that those models rely upon to "prove" their theories scientifically.

However, as Robert Wenzel has pointed out, Nobel Prize winner F.A. Hayek has already addressed this criticism and argued that economists should indeed use the deductive method, rather than an empirical one to understand economic principles. He even suggests that Robert Rubin would likely agree with Hayek's argument, because of what Rubin called "the very nature of reality--its complexity and ambiguity."

It is somewhat futile to try to win this argument with entrenched government policy makers. The Keynesian school advocates massive government intervention into the economy in order to protect us from the supposed shortcomings of the free market. When crises in the economy occur, the Keynesians recommend even greater intervention in the form of increased government spending, regulation, and monetary expansion.

The Austrian school advocates no government intervention into the economy at all. They argue that monumental crises are actually caused by intervention, so their cure is to cease whatever intervention has brought on the crisis, to relax regulations that impede adjustment in the labor market, and to allow the economy to rebalance itself through natural market forces.

Therefore, governments are not likely to reject Keynesianism, which grants them enormous power, and listen to the Austrians, who would strip it all away. One is reminded of the medieval governments that refused to acknowledge that the world was round and called upon appointed court scientists to legitimize their assertion that it was in fact flat.

However, it is important for investors to understand which theory within the “dismal science” truly does pass scientific muster. If you cannot dissuade the government from basing their policies on the wrong theory, you can at least choose the right one yourself to protect your own wealth and economic viability.

Anyone who has taken a basic chemistry class in high school remembers how you prove or disprove a theory. You conduct experiments to determine whether the predictions that your theory makes are correct. For example, your theory might predict that mixing two colorless chemicals in a test tube will result in the mixture turning blue. To prove it, you must not only conduct the experiment once, but over and over again, yielding the same result. If your test tube turns blue under the same conditions every time, you have proven your theory. If not, your theory is considered invalid and a new one must be formulated.

Austrian economists like F.A. Hayek predicted the Great Depression when the Keynesians said that the economy was fine. Once the crisis hit, the Austrians argued that the Keynesian policies prescribed to cure it would fail, as they were just an increase in the interventions that had caused the crisis in the first place. When massive government spending and devaluation of the currency failed to pull America out of the Depression, the Keynesians argued that more of the same to underwrite WWII would finally do the trick. Yet, the Depression lasted throughout the war and only subsided when it was over and there were massive cuts in government spending, consistent with the predictions of the Austrians.

The Keynesian answer to this anomaly? Ignore the results and just state that Keynesian policies did cure the Depression, regardless of indisputable facts to the contrary. This is science?

The Keynesians were also explicit that high unemployment and price inflation could never coexist together. The Austrians made no such claims, as they recognized that monetary expansion causes both price inflation and the malinvestment that leads to unemployment. In the 1970's, Austrian theory was again proven correct and Keynesian theory proven wrong.

Most recently, the Keynesians argued that the technology and housing bubbles were not bubbles at all, but sustainable increases in wealth caused by their wise stewardship of the economy. If you listened to them, you were either wiped out by the NASDAQ crash or left owning a house with an underwater mortgage, or both. If you listened to the Austrians, you got rid of your technology stocks early during the formation of the bubble and avoided buying houses whose price had been bid to unsustainable levels by the combination of monetary expansion and government intervention.

Even after all of this proof is in, the Keynesians are still employing the only defense they have left that their theory is sound. Deny, deny, deny. With government and consumer debt threatening to cause cataclysmic economic collapse, the Keynesians are encouraging government and consumers to borrow and spend more. The Austrians advise consumers to pay down their debts and investors to avoid the next bubble. They urge investors to protect their wealth in gold and other commodities, as they have for the past decade. Those that have listened to them have turned huge profits during this historic economic calamity.

Imagine that you are back in your high school chemistry class lab, conducting experiments. In the row behind you, an Austrian economist is testing his theory. The test tube turns blue one time after another, just as he predicted it would. In the row ahead, a Keynesian economist is testing his theory. His test tube turns a different color every time and then finally explodes, lighting his beard on fire. Which one would you deem the better scientist? Which one would you bet your life savings upon in the next experiment? If you wish to take the scientific approach, listen to the Austrians.

CHAPTER 11

NO ONE REALLY BELIEVES THE FEDERAL RESERVE

Originally published April 10, 2015

Last Friday was anything but good for news on the economy. The Bureau of Labor Statistics (BLS) released a dismal jobs report that missed expectations by fifty percent. This followed a press conference two weeks ago by Federal Reserve Chairman Janet Yellen during which she indicated rate hikes might not come as soon as expected because "room for further improvement in the labor market continues."

Yellen's statement would be fairly unremarkable if it were not for one troublesome fact: the U.S. economy is supposedly at "full employment," according to the measures the Fed uses to guide their interest rate policies. The Bureau of Labor Statistics has it at 5.5% as of today.[1] That is the rate most economists consider full employment for the U.S. economy and we've supposedly been there since February.

How could there be room for improvement in the labor market if we're at full employment? There can't be. But everybody knows real unemployment is much higher than the manipulated BLS statistics represent. Janet Yellen knows it. The markets know it. Tens of millions of unemployed Americans know it. Yet everyone keeps talking about the BLS unemployment rate as if it were true.

The BLS can stop counting your out-of-work brother-in-law as "unemployed" if he gives up looking for work, but that doesn't make him any more productive or him or anyone else any richer.

The other major index the Fed uses is just as phony. The BLS had core inflation at 1.7% for February.[2] Core inflation excludes food and energy prices, so falling crude oil and gasoline prices are not part of that number. If the core inflation number is accurate, then inflation is actually under the Fed's target rate of 2% per year. This is dangerous, according to a theory the Fed has pushed for over a decade. Inflation under 2% risks a deflationary depression.

If all of that is true, then why would the Fed even be considering raising interest rates, if it would be dangerous with the CPI at 1.7%?

The answer, of course, is that the CPI is just as phony as the unemployment rate and everyone knows that, too. Yellen knows it's phony. The markets know it's phony. And the millions of Americans paying higher prices for everything from school supplies to medical care know it's phony.

Incidentally, those plunging oil prices might not be a completely good thing. Yes, some part of the price deflation can be attributed to new supplies of oil, from fracking and new domestic discoveries. But are we supposed to believe there has been no drop in demand from those millions of not-technically-unemployed-but-still-not-actually-working Americans?

In reality, oil prices are acting a lot like they did

during the 1930s Depression.[3]

So, we've arrived at a bizarre place where a central bank supposedly bases its policies on government statistics it and everyone else knows are false. Nevertheless, the Fed goes through the motions of having meetings to pour over them and schedules press conferences to issue tortuously ambiguous statements on how these phony statistics are guiding its policy.

Then, regardless of what the statistics indicate, it just goes on inflating the currency at an unprecedented rate. That's because the Fed knows if it tightens, it's going to pop the bubble it's blown up and the phony recovery is going to come to a very abrupt and ugly halt.

Deep down, everyone else knows that, too. But no one wants to say it out loud. It's surreal.

In reality, we're in a depression. If we measured unemployment the way it was measured in the 1930s, it would look very similar to the 1930s. Food Stamps and HUD have replaced soup kitchens and Hoovervilles, but it's still a depression.

It had the same initial cause as the Great Depression: Federal Reserve inflation, followed by Federal Reserve deflation. It continues for the same reasons, too: Federal Reserve and federal government interventions have prevented the natural economic correction that would have occurred otherwise.

That's not the official story, but we all know it's true, just like we know unemployment isn't really 5.5%. What if we just admitted it?

What if we acknowledged the Fed has painted itself into a corner, with another crash virtually inevitable? What if we stopped believing the Fed was going to engineer some sort of "soft landing," even though it has never done so in its entire history? Would it help?

We can't avoid a correction in the markets. They're overvalued and should correct. We can't avoid the effects of the inflation the Fed has created or the massive government debt it has facilitated, either.

But we *can* at least resolve not to do the same thing after the next correction and expect a different result. Let's take the reins of the economy out of the Fed's hands and subject it to a full audit. A little reality can do nothing but help.

CHAPTER 12

I, INTEREST RATE

Originally published December 31, 2018

It is often said, "Don't kill the messenger," but that is precisely what everyone seems to want to do in my case. I'm not sure why because the news I bring is neither good nor bad. It is simply the truth; and it is a very sad day when telling the truth can foster such ill will. There are some who go so far as to declare my very existence wicked simply for providing information people use to engage in a specific type of voluntary exchange that, although of immense benefit to society, has somehow acquired an unsavory reputation.

As you may have surmised, I am the rate of interest,

the price difference between present goods and future goods. Now, many economists mistakenly identify me merely as the price of borrowing money over time, but that is only one of the many messages I carry. I also represent the price spread in the various stages of production, where capitalists purchase present goods in the form of factors of production in the hopes of selling what is produced for a higher price than what they spent. I am also this difference in price.

Nobody but me can gather the information I gather, for my message is determined by billions of individual transactions occurring simultaneously all over the economy. I consider the individual supply and demand schedules of hundreds of millions, sometimes billions of individual consumers and producers, along with the uncertainty involved in every time transaction, to determine the current price levels for transactions that involve time at any given moment.

In the case of individual borrowers, the uncertainty I mentioned includes that borrower's previous behavior, which is generally called a "credit rating."

The Usury Slander

While it is only one of the many prices I make available to the market, an inordinate amount of attention is paid to the price of borrowing money. That is likely for two reasons. One, as I said, is that most people erroneously believe it is the only information I impart. Two, people seem to be borrowing a lot more than they did previously in history for reasons I will explain shortly. As a result, it is regarding the price of borrowing money where I am most slandered and abused.

Because this price of borrowing is above zero, there are some who consider my existence alone evil. They say I'm a party to a crime they call "usury," which is a very strange concept. When everyone is acting honestly, money is a scarce commodity, so any loan by Person A to Person B requires a sacrifice on the part of A. Person A must forego consumption in the present in order to lend to B.

It is no different than if A were saving for a new car or

some other expensive item for himself. He must forego eating out as much, or buying new clothes, or going on vacation this year in order to put aside money to buy the expensive item next year.

By loaning money to B, A is allowing B to skip this sacrifice and purchase the expensive item now. It seems a very peculiar notion that A should forego spending his own money on himself only to let B use it for free when needed. How did this obligation to serve B free of charge come about? Aren't all men created equal?

Now, there are those who say it is not merely loaning money at interest but also charging exorbitantly high rates that constitutes usury. This makes no more sense than the previous definition. Is not the lender in every case charging a lower interest rate than any other willing lender for the given borrower? If that weren't true, the borrower would simply borrow from a lender offering a lower rate.

In fact, this so-called "usurer" may be the only lender willing to deal with the borrower in question at all. How can this make him a criminal or a sinner, while the rest who would charge higher rates or not make the loan at all are considered virtuous?

Regardless, it is not I who collects money from B or even imposes any obligation on B to pay A for the service. I am merely the messenger to both parties on what rate should be charged based on a plethora of information neither could possibly gather on his own.

Nobody Likes the Truth

Even many of those who don't believe charging interest is a crime are hostile to me. To them, I am like a friend who tells you the truth, rather than what you want to hear, but is not appreciated for doing so. Everyone wants me to proclaim a much lower rate than the conditions warrant.

Well, not everyone. Savers like higher interest rates. Borrowers like lower ones. There just seems to be more of the latter than the former these days, and they're a lot louder. So, forgive me if I sometimes think the borrowers represent everyone.

Borrowers are a diverse group. They include entrepreneurs seeking to expand production, consumers, and, of course, governments. This last group has two reasons for wanting me to lie.

First, they generally have borrowed large amounts of money in the past, resulting in an accumulated debt they cannot service at higher interest rates. Second, lower interest rates allow more borrowing by entrepreneurs to expand production. Expansion of production creates jobs, lowers unemployment, and makes society in general wealthier. Politicians generally take credit for the resulting higher standards of living, dubious as those claims generally are.

Unfortunately for them, I am incapable of lying directly. Current economic conditions at any given moment compel me to say what I say. I can no more change my message than any of you can cease being a human being. The politician, therefore, has developed a scheme to make me mislead market actors indirectly.

I said before that Person B's borrowing requires Person A's previous saving, *when everyone is acting honestly* and money is scarce. Let me first explain how things work under these conditions.

When there are relatively higher savings rates over the entire economy, meaning there is a decrease in consumption, the demand for goods and services is lower related to supply, and consumer prices fall. Inventories of tangible goods are temporarily accumulated. Profits for producers at the lowest stage of production decrease or they incur losses, giving them an incentive to switch investment from lower stages and seek greater returns on investments in higher stages of production.

This series of cause-effect relationships makes expanding the productive structure self-sustaining. The accumulated inventories and lower prices help sustain consumers while the supply of consumer goods being delivered is temporarily decreased. The accumulated savings help entrepreneurs complete the expansion of existing production and new projects they have launched. When these undertakings are completed, the productive structure is permanently larger, meaning more consumer goods per capita are produced. With more products produced, lower prices become permanent, and real wages rise. All of society is rendered richer.

How Central Banks Try to Make Me Lie

One would think it a perfectly reasonable proposition that consumption must decrease for production to expand. But for governments this is untenable. First, they seem completely incapable of decreasing their own consumption, no matter how large their deficits become. In addition, they have at least two reasons for not wanting their constituents to save.

One is they subscribe to a rather bizarre economic theory advanced by a school of economists who generally tell governments what they want to hear rather than the truth. Under this theory, wealth is created by consumption rather than production. When consumption falls, which I've just shown is the first necessary step toward expanding the productive structure, these economists say the government should override those millions or billions of individual decisions and spend more to offset what the public has not spent.

It isn't difficult to understand why proponents of this

theory would be heralded not only by governments but also by all those who wish for governments to expand in size and influence. They have constructed a theory that says government intervention into the economy is not only positive but vital to sustaining economic well-being. So, governments and these economists promote each other, working together to delegitimize any dissenting views.

The second reason governments resist the natural means for expanding production is they never want their constituents to experience even temporary, voluntary austerity. Having falsely taken credit for previous expansions, they don't want blame for temporary decreases in the supply of consumer goods even though it is necessary for long-term increases in supply. They want their constituents to believe they can "have their cake and eat it, too," and to take credit for this apparent economic miracle.

The chief impediment to promoting this fantasy is that money is scarce, when everyone is being honest. After all, one can't both consume a scarce commodity and retain possession of it at the same time. So, they have concocted a scheme under which money is not scarce.

At one time, every "Federal Reserve Note" was exchangeable for a defined amount of gold, the word "note" itself meaning the written record of a debt. Dollars at one time worked much like the ticket you get from the laundromat. You "deposit" one shirt, and the laundromat gives you a claim check. Later, you return the claim check and the laundromat gives you one shirt.

Dollars once operated the same way. One ounce of gold was deposited in the bank, and $20 was issued. If $20 were presented to the bank, the bank owed the bearer one ounce of gold, just as the laundromat owes you one shirt. Unlike the laundromat, however, you wouldn't get back the exact same ounce of gold initially deposited, as gold is fungible and shirts are not. Dollars were also exchangeable in the community for other items, without the gold ever moving from the bank vault. At any time, however, the current owner of your $20 was still entitled to exchange it at the bank for one ounce of gold.

As long as a certain amount of gold could be

demanded for each dollar in circulation, money remained scarce. Now, bankers would lend out more dollars than they could exchange for gold from time to time, either with or without the government's approval, as this greatly increased their earning potential. It was essentially a fraud, as the bank was loaning the same gold to one person it was legally obligated to pay on demand to another. Calling it "fractional reserve banking" made it sound technical and thereby more legitimate, but it was no less a fraud.

Fortunately, because of the risk that too many depositors might demand their gold at the same time, this expansion of the money supply beyond its gold backing was very limited.

To expand banks' ability to engage in this monetary inflation, the government created a central bank. At first, this central bank merely backstopped the rest of the banks under the same gold standard. But eventually, the exchangeability for gold was eliminated, making the name "Federal Reserve Note" an absurdity. After all, a piece of paper that cannot be exchanged for anything specific is no longer a "note" in financial terms. But it solved the problem of loaning the same dollar out to a borrower while making it simultaneously available for withdrawal to the depositor. Since neither could exchange it for any specific tangible item, both borrower and depositor could merrily go on pretending this arrangement was viable.

They say ignorance is bliss, although you all knowingly participate in this fraud today. So, it is more a case of believing what you want to believe.

Eliminating the gold standard allowed the central bank to create and destroy money arbitrarily for the general purpose of trying to make me lie to the public, encouraging them to make economic decisions the government wants them to make rather than decisions economic conditions deem prudent.

However, since it is impossible for me to lie - to announce a borrowing price based on anything other than current market conditions - central bankers must instead alter the conditions. When they announce they are going to "lower interest rates," what they really mean is they will increase the supply of money available to be lent. They accomplish this by purchasing securities, usually government bonds, from their member banks. In return for the securities, they give the member banks currency, created out of thin air.

As with an increase in available money due to savings, this monetary inflation decreases the price of borrowing, which in turn stimulates increased demand for borrowing. Governments borrow more; consumers borrow more; and entrepreneurs borrow more. This last group invests in higher order capital goods, expanding the productive structure just as they would if the increased money supply were due to savings. But it's not.

Since the expansion is not the result of savings, none of the consequences of saving that make expansion self-sustaining occur. Consumption does not decrease, lowering the demand for consumer goods. So, consumer goods prices don't fall. They either rise, stay the same, or fall less than they would have without the monetary inflation. Inventories are not built up. Overall, the lower prices, inventories, and cash on hand resulting from savings are not there to sustain the economy while entrepreneurs expand production.

Eventually, to combat the rising consumer goods prices they have stimulated by increasing the money supply, the central bank must decrease the money supply. They do this by selling securities back to their member banks in exchange for money. This lowers the amount of money available to be lent out to the rest of the economy, which increases the price of borrowing.

When this cycle ends badly, I get all the blame. Politicians especially claim stock market crashes and economic depressions are the result of “interest rates being raised too high or too quickly,” as if it is merely my telling the truth that causes all the economic problems.

Obviously, that’s not true. The problem isn’t what I tell markets but the bad decisions previously made by market actors based on artificially-created conditions. Entrepreneurs begin higher order production projects when the savings required to finish them are not there. They choose to start these projects under false pretenses, even if they are not consciously aware of it. While they may base their decisions purely on lower interest rates, lower rates are normally accompanied by savings, lower consumer goods prices, and inventories. That makes my message a reliable signal for investment decisions. Lower rates based on monetary inflation are not.

Consumers have also borrowed more based on the artificially lower rates. They took on debt burdens they would not have under natural market conditions when only their savings could have produced the lower interest rate in the first place. After all, one cannot consume more and less at the same time. And since they haven't lowered their consumption, they don't have the benefit of the lower consumer goods prices they would have enjoyed if expansion of production was fueled by their savings.

Not only consumer goods prices, but the prices of all goods increase when the money supply is increased, other things being equal. The prices of stocks and houses are especially vulnerable to being bid up to artificially high levels.

Overall, capital is expended on producing capital goods for projects that won't ultimately be profitable. When these projects are abandoned, any capital expended on capital goods that can't be repurposed has been wasted, making society permanently poorer than it would otherwise have been.

Massive labor resources are also dedicated to these doomed projects. When the projects are abandoned, these people all lose their jobs. While they eventually can move to other projects, they are unemployed until new projects are launched and any new training they require is completed. While unemployed, they suffer personal hardship and the rest of society is rendered poorer than if they were productively employed.

Compounding the calamity is the opportunity cost of all these losses. Had labor and capital not been misdirected by artificially lower interest rates, all the misdirected resources would have been employed productively. All they would have produced during the artificial boom and subsequent bust represents another permanent loss to society.

It goes without saying that I abhor being even an involuntary party to any of this reprehensible behavior. And I must reiterate that the central bank has never made me lie outright. My price message to borrowers and lenders was perfectly accurate, based on the money supply conditions at every stage. It was the way those conditions were created by the central bank—from new fiat money creation rather than savings—that caused all the problems.

Be Honest with Me and Yourselves

As I tell my story, it seems that yet another economic calamity looms. Already, I can hear my name being dragged through the mud as a party to the scheme that caused it. While I'm unjustly being pronounced guilty by association, many other innocent parties will be scapegoated to direct attention away from the real culprits, the government and its central bank. Supposed "deregulation," lower taxes, and even the free market itself will be blamed.

Blaming the free market is especially despicable given that overriding market conditions with monetary inflation, resulting in interest rates lower than what the market would have me prescribe, is what caused the bubble in the first place.

Nevertheless, after creating the disease by overriding the market, politicians and central bankers will demand it be overridden again as the market tries to administer the cure—falling asset prices, bankruptcies, abandonment of non-profitable enterprises for profitable ones, and liquidation of debt. Instead, the central bank will use more monetary inflation to prop up stock and housing prices, sustain bad debt, and continue unprofitable businesses. Then, the cycle will start all over again.

What can be done? As always, I will tell you the truth, even if you don't want to hear it. Fix your monetary system. I don't particularly care if your currency is backed by gold, diamonds, or some other scarce, fungible commodity. It need only be naturally scarce, its supply not subject to anyone's whim, no matter how public-spirited or "independent" they claim to be.

Get rid of your central bank. Your country got along

fine for 90 of your 243 years without one. In fact, your previous two central banks had a hand in causing the crises cited as the excuse to create your present one. When the government breaks your leg, you're better off letting it heal than accepting the government's crutch.

After getting rid of your central bank, don't let the remaining independent banks lend out more money than they have. That's the real root of the problem whether a central bank is there to exacerbate it or not. Don't fall for the canard fractional reserve banking is necessary for growth to occur quickly enough. Bubbles aren't real growth.

Don't make scapegoats of the bankers, either. You know they're operating on a fractional reserve. As much as they want to generate revenues based on loaning money they don't really have, you want to earn interest on money you know they've loaned out. Please be honest with yourselves and me.

Obviously, enforcing these disciplines will necessitate much less government spending, but that shouldn't bother anyone. The government shuts down from time to time, and nobody really notices. Certainly, no sane person would argue a government running trillion-dollar deficits can afford non-essential personnel. Those should be the first costs cut, but there are plenty more.

No matter what you decide, I will go on telling you the truth; I can do nothing else. Now that you know I merely communicate a price level based on supply, demand, and uncertainty, you know it is how those underlying economic conditions are determined—naturally or artificially—that determines your economic fate. You can go on doing the same thing you are doing now—lying to yourselves and trying to get me to do the same—but you shouldn't expect different results. Someone once said that's the definition of insanity.

CHAPTER 13

EVERYONE SHOULD WANT TO END THE FED

Ironically, both conservatives and socialists could claim the Federal Reserve as their own. Alexander Hamilton and Karl Marx were both proponents of a central bank, for different reasons.

Along with government infrastructure and high protectionist tariffs, the central bank was a chief plank of not only Hamilton's Federalists, but the Whig Party that replaced them and the Republican Party that replaced the Whigs. The Federal Reserve Act was signed into law by Democratic President Woodrow Wilson, but it was really a creature of the Republican Party, only slightly tweaked by Wilson and the Democrats in 1913.

Plank #5 of the Communist Manifesto is, "Centralisation of credit in the hands of the State, by means of a national bank with State capital and an exclusive monopoly." Marx and Engels believed establishing a central bank controlled by the government would be one key in transferring capital from the few to the many. This is just one of many things they were completely wrong about.

Regardless, it would not have been a key plank in the most famous plan in history to eliminate capitalism if it were a capitalist institution. And by "capitalism," I mean private property and laissez faire markets. The word was made popular by Marx and Engels as a pejorative, who used it to describe both free markets *and* elements not necessarily part of that system. But today it is universally understood to mean a free market system, although even capitalism's proponents today often mistake anti-capitalist institutions for capitalist ones. This couldn't be truer than for the Fed.

Why the Left should oppose the Fed

Regardless of what you call it, it is clear the Fed is a wealth transfer scheme, whether intentionally or not, in precisely the wrong direction for the left. In fact, the absence of a central bank between 1837 and 1912 was one of the reasons there was no proletariat revolution in the United States.

The overall reason is something the left doesn't want to hear: the Industrial Revolution raised the living standards of working-class people exponentially. Contrary to Marx's prediction, there was no "crisis of capitalism" where wages were driven so low the workers could no longer afford to purchase the products they made. Instead, wages rose and consumer goods prices fell as productivity increased, increasing *real wages* dramatically. The price deflation that occurred under the monetary discipline of the gold standard during the Industrial Revolution was a crucial component of this phenomenon.

Two stories the left should be especially interested in are Elizabeth Keckley's and Mary Ann Magnin's. Keckley was born a slave and eventually bought her and her son's freedom with money saved from being a seamstress. Magnin was born free to modest circumstances, but also used savings accumulated from sewing to significantly improve her economic condition. She opened a clothing store that she eventually grew to a business with locations up and down the west coast.[1]

These remarkable stories of successful women in a male-dominated society were only possible because the money they earned and saved retained its value. It isn't quite impossible for low-income earners to save and start a business with our present system, but it's much, much harder. More sacrifice is required, and all the incentives are wrong.

It goes without saying that price inflation itself hurts low-income earners the most. Yes, a dramatic increase in the price of gasoline, for example, hurts Amazon's profits and, in theory, decreases its stock value and Jeff Bezos's net worth. But it devastates the people making $15 per hour, for whom gasoline represents a much larger percentage of living expenses. In addition, the raise in Amazon's or Walmart's operating expenses raises the costs of things hourly workers buy, compounding the increase in their living expenses.

Economists would say it lowers their "real wages." In plain English, it makes them poorer.

Even without corrupt bailouts of the rich like TARP, the system works against capital accumulation in low-income earners. Yes, monetary inflation raises wages *eventually*. But it always keeps the prices of products just a little ahead of wages. By depressing interest rates, it makes savings accounts a losing proposition, since the interest earned is less than the purchasing power lost to price inflation.

More destructive still to low-income earners is the malinvestment monetary inflation encourages. During the inevitable price deflations that occur during busts like 2008, low-income earners are the most likely to lose their jobs and wipe out what savings they'd managed to accumulate. That is, if they hadn't been tempted into too much debt by the same artificially low interest rates that caused the malinvestment in the first place. In that case, they're merely struggling to pay off debt while the investor class swoops in to gobble up assets at deflated prices.

There is a popular narrative that says income and wealth inequality increased rapidly since the 1980s, due to the “deregulation” and other pro-business policies of President Ronald Reagan. There is only one problem: the trend began in the 1970s, before Reagan was elected.[2]

Anyone who lived through the 1970s is aware there was no laissez faire revolution during either the Nixon, Ford, or Carter administrations. But there was one significant economic policy that changed: the decoupling of the U.S. dollar from gold in August 1971.

The dollar had not been exchangeable for gold within the United States since the New Deal, but per the Bretton Woods agreement, foreign central banks were still allowed to trade their acquired dollars for gold at an exchange rate of $35.00 per ounce. When those central banks began to suspect the U.S. government could not make good on this promise due to the Fed’s monetary inflation in support of “guns and butter” spending on the Vietnam War and LBJ’s Great Society, they began to trade their dollars for gold at an accelerated rate.

Nixon's closing of the gold window was followed by significant price inflation throughout the decade, prompting his administration to impose wage and price controls. By 1979, inflation had risen to 11.3%, peaking at 13.5% the following year. Reagan was not elected until November 1980 and didn't take office until January 1981. Rather than the Reagan years, it was this period of runaway price inflation, caused by previous monetary inflation, that marked the beginning of the trend of increasing income and wealth inequality.

Why did this trend continue after price inflation was broken with high interest rates imposed by Fed Chairman Paul Voelker? It certainly wasn't Reagan's minimal deregulation. Reagan talked a good game for fans of small government, but federal spending doubled while he was president. The more significant development during Reagan's presidency was the now-infamous "Greenspan put."

This refers to the Federal Reserve policy, begun after the 1987 stock market crash, of flooding the economy with cash in response to a crisis. This created the moral hazard that the Federal Reserve will bail out investors when markets go down. This essentially "privatizes profits and socializes losses," since the new money in effect transfers purchasing power from everyone to the investment class.

Americans have lived through a replay of this transfer during every correction since, including the NASDAQ crash of 2000, the 2008 housing bubble meltdown, and the Covid crash. Between crashes, the upward wealth transfer slows from a monsoon to a trickle, but it never stops.

Does this sound like a more persuasive argument for why income and wealth inequality skyrocketed beginning in the 1970s than the unremarkable policies of a big-spending Republican president in the 1980s?

The past 50 years have seen vast expansions of government welfare programs that have not even slowed the income and wealth inequality trend over the same period. As with Trump supporters, I ask all on the left unhappy with this trend to be honest with themselves. More of what didn't work, financed by Federal Reserve monetary inflation, isn't going to suddenly start working. Instead, the left should focus on the root of the problem and demand we end the Fed.

Why the Right should oppose the Fed

What set Donald Trump apart from other recent Republican presidential candidates was his willingness to discard libertarianish talk about the free market (and it was mostly just talk) and promise to get America out of the free trade deals which had destroyed American manufacturing and created the "American Carnage" he described in his inaugural address.

Trump tapped into a genuine belief that American manufacturing had been decimated and the high-paying factory jobs it provided had been exported overseas to China, Mexico, and other low wage jurisdictions. Trump promised to bring those jobs back by renegotiating NAFTA and imposing tariffs on foreign imports.

There are two things wrong with this worldview. One, the claim American manufacturing had been decimated is grossly exaggerated and what damage had been done was done by the Federal Reserve, not trade deals. Two, the tariffs Trump imposed did not revive American manufacturing overall. In fact, they sent it into a recession.

Those claims may be startling to Trump supporters, so let's look at the data. Now, it is true that manufacturing jobs had been declining for decades when Trump ran in 2016, but not because of NAFTA or China entering the World Trade Organization (WTO). Here is a chart of manufacturing jobs as a percentage of all U.S. jobs since 1947:

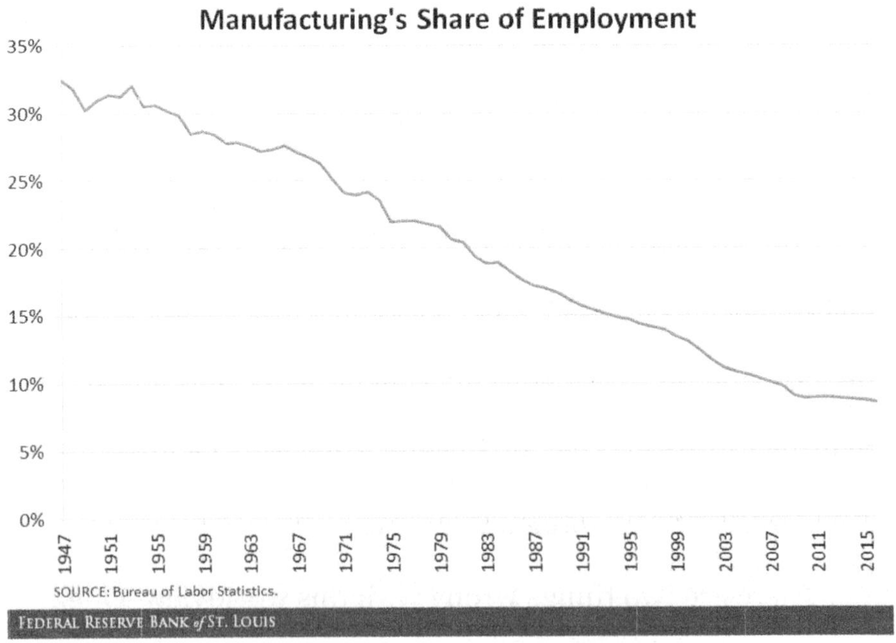

Source: Federal Reserve of St. Louis (reprinted from Bureau of Labor Statistics) https://www.stlouisfed.org/on-the-economy/2017/april/us-manufacturing-really-declining

As you can see, manufacturing jobs as a percentage of all jobs has been declining steadily since 1947. But there is no acceleration of the trend after NAFTA (1994) or China entering the WTO (2000). In fact, the decline decelerates after 2009.

Moreover, the decline in manufacturing jobs isn't due to a decline in manufacturing *output*. Here is a chart of output for the past one hundred years:

Source: Macrotrends https://www.macrotrends.net/2583/industrial-production-historical-chart

These data do not support the argument manufacturing output was significantly impacted by either NAFTA or China entering the WTO. Output continued to make new highs after both. But notice where there are temporary declines: in 1999, the year before the NASDAQ crash, in 2007, the year before the housing meltdown, and in 2018.

2018 is an outlier in that it is the same year as a stock market correction but precedes the big crash of 2020 by more than two years. But 2018 is noteworthy for another reason: Trump's tariffs.

Economists consider the ISM Manufacturing Index a health indicator of the manufacturing sector. Any value below 50 is considered to indicate the sector is in a recession. Below is a snapshot of the index for 2012 – 2021.

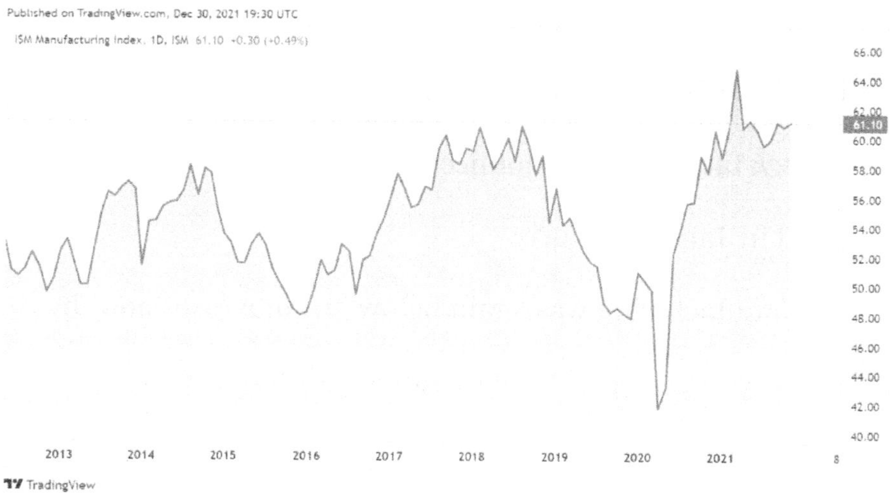

Source: TradingView.com

https://www.tradingview.com/chart/?symbol=ISM%3AMAN_PMI

As you can see, manufacturing fell into recession territory in December 2015, followed by a rally that saw it rise through 2016, fall back briefly below 50 in August 2016, and from there begin another rally that peaked in September 2017 (with slightly higher highs in 2018 amidst sideways movement). This all occurred prior to the imposition of tariffs, which began in early 2018 but did not reach full force until June 2018.[3]

The ISM shows manufacturing plummeted immediately afterwards, reaching recession levels by July 2019. It bottomed and began a recovery in November 2019, just as the "Phase One Trade Deal" with China, which promised to *rollback* tariffs, was announced.[4] The deal was eventually signed in January 2020.[5]

Manufacturing was again below 50 (in a recession) by February 2020, *before* the Covid-19 pandemic measures were put in place. Following the Covid recession, the index briefly soared above 64 before returning to 61, a routine high for the index since 1988.

None of this fits the economic nationalism narrative. If the trade deals had any significant effect on either manufacturing jobs or manufacturing output, we'd see it on the corresponding charts. We don't. Likewise, if the tariffs helped "restore" American manufacturing, we would not see it fall into a recession while the highest tariffs were in place and recover to relative normality after the harshest tariffs were removed.

The narrative that does fit the data is manufacturing jobs have been declining while output has been increasing for the same reasons as farm jobs: the U.S. simply got much more efficient at manufacturing. Automation explains most of the job losses.

That doesn't mean that some manufacturing jobs didn't move to China. With four times the population, China has a huge comparative advantage in labor over the United States. It would make sense that labor-intensive manufacturing would move to China, just as it makes sense that the U.S. would be a net exporter of agricultural products due to its huge comparative advantage in productive farmland (China has more land mass but a relative dearth of good farmland).

Nevertheless, China entering the WTO had no discernible effect on U.S. manufacturing output, which kept on increasing at the same rate afterwards. The U.S. simply continued to produce more with less people as it had been doing since 1947.

What did have an effect on manufacturing output was the financial crisis of 2008. Manufacturing declined sharply starting in December 2007 and did not regain its previous high until 2014. It has again plummeted as a result of the

Covid recession and as of August 2021 was only back to 2013 levels.

Whether the Covid recession can be considered an anomaly or simply covered a Federal Reserve business cycle bust that would have happened in 2020 anyway is a matter of speculation. What can be concluded from the data is that the trade deals did not harm U.S. manufacturing, but the economic boom-bust cycles caused by the Federal Reserve did. If anything, freer trade resulting in lower-priced consumer goods probably helped middle class Americans by muting the price inflation effects of the unprecedented monetary inflation that has been a consistent feature throughout the 21st century, especially after 2009.

Even the trade deficit, which is vastly exaggerated as an economic problem, reflects the ills of monetary inflation. President Trump characterized the trade deficit as money the U.S. was "losing" to foreign trading partners. But nobody wins or loses in a voluntary exchange or the "loser" wouldn't agree to the trade in the first place. As Adam Smith wrote in his seminal *Wealth of Nations*,

> Nothing, however, can be more absurd than this whole doctrine of the balance of trade, upon which, not only these restraints, but almost all the other regulations of commerce are founded. When two places trade with one another, this doctrine supposes that, if the balance be even, neither of them either loses or gains; but if it leans in any degree to one side, that one of them loses and the other gains in proportion to its declension from the exact equilibrium.[6]

When the U.S. imports more products from China than it exports to China, it does not by itself indicate a problem. Neither does the aggregate trade deficit in any given year indicate a problem. However, one would expect to see an ebb and flow of trade deficits and surpluses over long periods of time. But the U.S. has had persistent trade deficits and this is indicative of a concern, but not with bad trade deals.

First, let's put the trade deficits in perspective. In 2019, the overall trade deficit of the U.S. was $616 billion.[7]

That might sound like a whopping number, but U.S. GDP for that year was $21,433 trillion (after deducting the trade deficit). That means the trade deficit represented about 2% of all trade, domestic and international, that occurred in the United States in 2019.

Rather than a massive loss, the trade deficit is indicative of the country as a whole producing quite a bit but consuming just a little more than it produced. This is precisely what monetary inflation and its effect on interest rates encourages. Artificially low interest rates encourage borrowing to consume and discourage saving to invest.

Monetary inflation and the malinvestment it causes harms the manufacturing sector especially severely. It props up zombie firms and whole industries the market would otherwise liquidate, redirecting the capital they are consuming towards more productive ends. And it encourages everyone to consume more than they produce, borrowing the difference at artificially low interest rates, rather than accumulate savings that can serve as capital for expansion of productive capacity. These all represent massive waste of resources that otherwise might flow towards investment in more productive activities, including manufacturing.

Making American consumers pay more for the same goods with tariffs leaves even less money left over for savings, the only true source of capital investment for expansion of productive capacity. The right should cease supporting destructive trade wars and instead demand we end the Fed.

Wouldn't Ending the Fed Result in Chaos?

The media attempted to paint Ron Paul as a "kook" while he was running for president. Hopefully, both Donald Trump and Bernie Sanders supporters have developed a healthy skepticism of the national media since then.

One "nutty" thing Ron Paul said all the way back in 2001 was that the housing bubble the Federal Reserve was blowing up in response to the NASDAQ meltdown (the result of a previous Fed bubble) was going to end badly. He also predicted in 2011 that if the U.S. did not leave Afghanistan, we would be there for another ten years.[8] He added in 2013 that the Taliban would end up back in control either way.[9]

“Why should we listen to this guy?” he asks sarcastically.

Paul’s recommendation for ending the Fed isn’t to close it down immediately. Instead, he proposes stricter regulations on what the Fed is allowed to do, such as prohibitions on bailouts and debt monetization, while legalizing competing currencies. By “legalizing,” he means removing sales and capital gains taxes from currencies that compete with the U.S. dollar. Paul focused on gold and silver back in 2009, but there is no reason this exemption couldn’t be extended to cryptocurrencies or other currency alternatives.

These taxes don’t comprise a substantial percentage of federal revenue. They are there simply to protect the dollar’s monopoly. That the dollar would need this protection should tell you something is fishy about it. Giving it competition would both protect Americans from the wealth transfer inherent in monetary inflation and impose market discipline on the dollar. The Fed would either have to stop inflating or see consumers cease using its currency.

But since overriding the market decisions of individuals through inflation is the whole reason for having a Federal Reserve System in the first place, competition would mean the eventual end of the Fed. Competing currencies would simply accomplish it with less disruption than would abrupt abolition.

Ironically, it was market competition in currency that led to the U.S. dollar in the first place. The dollar was created in 1792 based upon the Spanish silver dollar, which emerged from a free market in coins during the colonial years and early years of the American republic.

If you've ever heard 25 cents referred to as, "two bits," it's because the Spanish dollar was often literally cut up into eight bits ("pieces of eight") for smaller denomination transactions. Two of these bits equaled a quarter dollar. The expression stuck around in America well after the Spanish silver dollar ceased to be used as currency.

So, there is nothing radical or unprecedented about competing currencies. It was the norm in early America and directly led to the establishment of the U.S. dollar. The

Coinage Act of 1792 defined the dollar "to contain three hundred and seventy-one grains and four sixteenth parts of a grain of pure, or four hundred and sixteen grains of standard silver."[10] Larger denomination coins were defined in fixed amounts of gold.

The Fed Makes Government All-Powerful

As economist Robert Murphy relates, the original dollar was not a paper currency backed by gold or silver, but exclusively the coins themselves.[11] The power "To coin Money, regulate the Value thereof" given to the federal government in the U.S. Constitution refers to the creation of coins out of gold or silver bullion, and the power exercised in the Coinage Act to define how much gold or silver would comprise a dollar.

This has nothing to do with banking or issuing currency like Federal Reserve Notes, a power nowhere delegated to the government in the Constitution. This is why Thomas Jefferson fiercely opposed the First Bank of the United States, which had nothing like the power the Federal Reserve wields today. James Madison left the Federalist

Party and joined Jefferson in founding the original Republican Party (called "Democratic-Republicans" by historians) for the same reason.

Since this was before the Supreme Court "discovered" its power of judicial review, the final decision of whether the national bank was Constitutional rested with Congress and the president. Dominated by the Federalist Party, the bill creating the bank easily passed Congress. President Washington asked both Alexander Hamilton and Thomas Jefferson to give him written opinions on its constitutionality. After considering them, Washington deferred to his treasury secretary.

Hamilton argued for the bank based on the novel concept of "implied powers" in the Constitution, even though the delegates who ratified the Constitution had been told the government would only exercise powers "expressly delegated."[12] The national bank's constitutionality would later be affirmed by the Supreme Court in *McCulloch v. Maryland*, pertaining to the Second Bank of the United

States, signed into law by none other than President James Madison.

Now, if you believe the Supreme Court is always correct in its determination of what is and is not constitutional, you can rest assured the federal government is delegated the power to incorporate a bank and issue currency. For strict constructionists, the national banks and the Federal Reserve System that followed them are not only unconstitutional, but the original departure from the Constitution's limits on federal power that opened the Pandora's Box of all that followed.

Regardless of its constitutionality, the Federal Reserve System is an economically destructive institution that not only transfers wealth to the richest one percent and causes the boom-bust cycle, but also removes all restraint on government. Everything the government does costs money. So, the more money it has at its disposal, the more powerful it becomes.

There is no way Covid lockdowns could have occurred without the Fed. Without the new money created out of thin air by the Fed and doled out by the federal government, far more states would have responded to the Covid pandemic the way Iowa, Florida, South Dakota, and Texas did (with no significant difference in outcomes).

Not only did the Fed make the lockdowns possible; it created an even bigger problem for Americans going forward. Below is a chart of the M2 money supply:

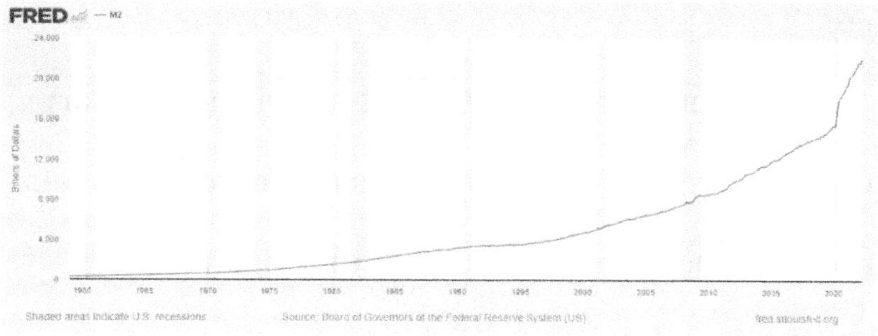

Source: Federal Reserve Bank of St. Louis

https://fred.stlouisfed.org/series/M2NS#

*A previous edition cited M1 here, which was redefined in early 2021 in a way that made the graphical representation confusing as to money creation during 2020-22.

The monetary inflation employed to underwrite the Covid lockdowns dwarfs even Quantitative Easing in scale. It put almost half as much money in circulation in one year as had been created in the previous 107 years the Fed had existed. 30 percent of all dollars are now dollars created since March 2020. If you thought the 2008 financial crisis was bad, this has the potential for a catastrophe far worse.

The Fed promises to fight the price inflation we're already seeing by beginning its "tapering" plan sooner than previously planned. Tapering isn't decreasing the money supply; it's merely inflating at a slower pace. That's obviously not going to work given the tsunami of money that's already out there.

The problem facing the Fed is its previous monetary inflation had already blown up bubbles in the stock markets, education, healthcare, and housing. If they tighten significantly, those bubbles are going to pop. If they don't, price inflation is going to rage for years.

To the extent resources are currently malinvested due to monetary inflation, a recession is necessary to redirect those resources to productive use. But it's going to be painful, maybe the most painful recession in history.

We shouldn't be in this position, and we don't have to be. It is only the central bank that makes possible disasters like the Covid lockdowns, dumb, endless wars, skyrocketing health and education costs, welfare for billionaires, and catastrophic meltdowns.

This is all financed by government debt that is only possible because of the Federal Reserve. Every dollar the government borrows is a dollar that has been directed away from productive use. Every bond it issues crowds out a corporate bond, representing borrowed funds that could have been used to expand production rather than on boondoggles like the Afghanistan War or the "shovel ready" projects of the American Recovery and Reinvestment Act of 2009. It is only because of the Federal Reserve that federal debt has grown from $424 billion in 1971 to over $28 trillion in 2021 – a staggering 67-fold increase.

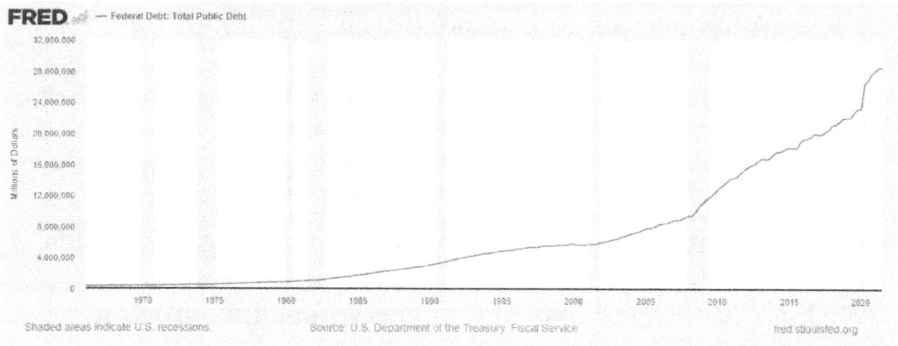

Source: Federal Reserve Bank of St. Louis https://fred.stlouisfed.org/series/GFDEBTN/

Obviously, this is unsustainable. But the Biden administration is calling for even more debt-fueled government spending while simultaneously claiming the economy is doing great. Not even the Keynesians would call that a good idea. Just imagine what the administration will want to do when the next recession hits.

It's too late to escape the effects of the money blizzard the Fed loosed on the economy over the past two years. We will have to suffer through a recession at some point to correct all the malinvestment it caused. The best we can hope for is a federal government that won't make it even worse by responding to the next bust with even more wasteful spending.

What we can do is make the current boom-bust cycle our last. Starting in 2022, demand the politicians you elect start the process to end the Federal Reserve System by reigning in its powers and legalizing competing currencies. We have nothing to lose but an enormous, incompetent, tyrannical government and a distorted economy rigged to benefit the wealthy at the expense of everyone else.

Appendix A – Price Inflation Rates 1800-2019

Year	Inflation Rate	Basket of Goods
1800		$100.00
1801	-2.00%	$98.00
1802	-14.00%	$84.28
1803	4.70%	$88.24
1804	0.00%	$88.24
1805	0.00%	$88.24
1806	4.40%	$92.12
1807	-6.40%	$86.23
1808	9.10%	$94.07
1809	-2.10%	$92.10
1810	0.00%	$92.10
1811	6.40%	$97.99
1812	2.00%	$99.95
1813	13.70%	$113.65
1814	8.60%	$123.42
1815	-12.70%	$107.75
1816	-7.30%	$99.88
1817	-5.90%	$93.99
1818	-4.20%	$90.04
1819	0.00%	$90.04
1820	-8.70%	$82.21
1821	-4.80%	$78.26
1822	0.00%	$78.26
1823	-10.00%	$70.43
1824	-8.30%	$64.59
1825	3.00%	$66.53
1826	0.00%	$66.53
1827	0.00%	$66.53
1828	-2.90%	$64.60
1829	-3.00%	$62.66
1830	0.00%	$62.66
1831	0.00%	$62.66

1832	-6.30%	$58.71
1833	-3.30%	$56.77
1834	3.40%	$58.70
1835	3.30%	$60.64
1836	6.50%	$64.58
1837	3.00%	$66.52
1838	-5.90%	$62.60
1839	0.00%	$62.60
1840	-6.30%	$58.65
1841	3.30%	$60.59
1842	-6.50%	$56.65
1843	-3.40%	$54.72
1844	0.00%	$54.72
1845	0.00%	$54.72
1846	-3.60%	$52.75
1847	3.70%	$54.71
1848	-7.10%	$50.82
1849	-3.80%	$48.89
1850	0.00%	$48.89
1851	0.00%	$48.89
1852	0.00%	$48.89
1853	0.00%	$48.89
1854	8.00%	$52.80
1855	3.70%	$54.76
1856	-3.60%	$52.78
1857	3.70%	$54.74
1858	-7.10%	$50.85
1859	3.80%	$52.78
1860	0.00%	$52.78
1861	0.00%	$52.78
1862	11.10%	$58.64
1863	23.30%	$72.31
1864	27.00%	$91.83
1865	-2.10%	$89.90
1866	-4.30%	$86.03

1867	-4.50%	$82.16
1868	-4.80%	$78.22
1869	0.00%	$78.22
1870	-5.00%	$74.31
1871	-5.30%	$70.37
1872	0.00%	$70.37
1873	0.00%	$70.37
1874	-5.60%	$66.43
1875	-2.90%	$64.50
1876	-3.00%	$62.57
1877	0.00%	$62.57
1878	-9.40%	$56.69
1879	-3.40%	$54.76
1880	3.60%	$56.73
1881	0.00%	$56.73
1882	0.00%	$56.73
1883	-3.40%	$54.80
1884	-3.60%	$52.83
1885	0.00%	$52.83
1886	0.00%	$52.83
1887	0.00%	$52.83
1888	0.00%	$52.83
1889	0.00%	$52.83
1890	0.00%	$52.83
1891	0.00%	$52.83
1892	0.00%	$52.83
1893	0.00%	$52.83
1894	-3.70%	$50.87
1895	-3.80%	$48.94
1896	0.00%	$48.94
1897	0.00%	$48.94
1898	0.00%	$48.94
1899	0.00%	$48.94
1900	0.00%	$48.94
1901	0.00%	$48.94

1902	4.00%	$50.90
1903	3.80%	$52.83
1904	0.00%	$52.83
1905	0.00%	$52.83
1906	0.00%	$52.83
1907	3.70%	$54.79
1908	-3.60%	$52.81
1909	0.00%	$52.81
1910	3.70%	$54.77
1911	0.00%	$54.77
1912	3.60%	$56.74
1913	**2.40%**	**$58.10**
1914	1.30%	$58.86
1915	0.90%	$59.39
1916	7.70%	$63.96
1917	17.80%	$75.34
1918	17.30%	$88.38
1919	15.20%	$101.81
1920	15.60%	$117.70
1921	-10.90%	$104.87
1922	-6.20%	$98.37
1923	1.80%	$100.14
1924	0.40%	$100.54
1925	2.40%	$102.95
1926	0.90%	$103.88
1927	-1.90%	$101.90
1928	-1.20%	$100.68
1929	0.00%	$100.68
1930	-2.70%	$97.96
1931	-8.90%	$89.24
1932	-10.30%	$80.05
1933	-5.20%	$75.89
1934	3.50%	$78.54
1935	2.60%	$80.59
1936	1.00%	$81.39

1937	3.70%	$84.40
1938	-2.00%	$82.72
1939	-1.30%	$81.64
1940	0.70%	$82.21
1941	5.10%	$86.40
1942	10.90%	$95.82
1943	6.00%	$101.57
1944	1.60%	$103.20
1945	2.30%	$105.57
1946	8.50%	$114.54
1947	14.40%	$131.04
1948	7.70%	$141.13
1949	-1.00%	$139.72
1950	1.10%	$141.25
1951	7.90%	$152.41
1952	2.30%	$155.92
1953	0.80%	$157.17
1954	0.30%	$157.64
1955	-0.30%	$157.16
1956	1.50%	$159.52
1957	3.30%	$164.79
1958	2.70%	$169.24
1959	1.00%	$170.93
1960	1.50%	$173.49
1961	1.10%	$175.40
1962	1.20%	$177.50
1963	1.20%	$179.63
1964	1.30%	$181.97
1965	1.60%	$184.88
1966	3.00%	$190.43
1967	2.80%	$195.76
1968	4.30%	$204.18
1969	5.50%	$215.41
1970	5.80%	$227.90
1971	4.30%	$237.70

1972	3.30%	$245.55
1973	6.20%	$260.77
1974	11.10%	$289.71
1975	9.10%	$316.08
1976	5.70%	$334.09
1977	6.50%	$355.81
1978	7.60%	$382.85
1979	11.30%	$426.11
1980	13.50%	$483.64
1981	10.30%	$533.46
1982	6.10%	$566.00
1983	3.20%	$584.11
1984	4.30%	$609.22
1985	3.50%	$630.55
1986	1.90%	$642.53
1987	3.70%	$666.30
1988	4.10%	$693.62
1989	4.80%	$726.91
1990	5.40%	$766.17
1991	4.20%	$798.35
1992	3.00%	$822.30
1993	3.00%	$846.97
1994	2.60%	$868.99
1995	2.80%	$893.32
1996	2.90%	$919.22
1997	2.30%	$940.37
1998	1.60%	$955.41
1999	2.20%	$976.43
2000	3.40%	$1,009.63
2001	2.80%	$1,037.90
2002	1.60%	$1,054.51
2003	2.30%	$1,078.76
2004	2.70%	$1,107.89
2005	3.40%	$1,145.55
2006	3.20%	$1,182.21

2007	2.90%	$1,216.50
2008	3.80%	$1,262.72
2009	-0.40%	$1,257.67
2010	1.60%	$1,277.79
2011	3.20%	$1,318.68
2012	2.10%	$1,346.38
2013	1.50%	$1,366.57
2014	1.60%	$1,388.44
2015	0.10%	$1,389.83
2016	1.30%	$1,407.89
2017	2.10%	$1,437.46
2018	2.40%	$1,471.96
2019*	1.80%	$1,498.45

Source: Federal Reserve Bank of Minneapolis https://www.minneapolisfed.org/about-us/monetary-policy/inflation-calculator/consumer-price-index-1800-

Appendix B Unemployment Rates 1948-2021

Year	Jan	Feb	Mar	Apr	May	Jun	Jul	Aug	Sep	Oct	Nov	Dec
1948	3.4	3.8	4.0	3.9	3.5	3.6	3.6	3.9	3.8	3.7	3.8	4.0
1949	4.3	4.7	5.0	5.3	6.1	6.2	6.7	6.8	6.6	7.9	6.4	6.6
1950	6.5	6.4	6.3	5.8	5.5	5.4	5.0	4.5	4.4	4.2	4.2	4.3
1951	3.7	3.4	3.4	3.1	3.0	3.2	3.1	3.1	3.3	3.5	3.5	3.1
1952	3.2	3.1	2.9	2.9	3.0	3.0	3.2	3.4	3.1	3.0	2.8	2.7
1953	2.9	2.6	2.6	2.7	2.5	2.5	2.6	2.7	2.9	3.1	3.5	4.5
1954	4.9	5.2	5.7	5.9	5.9	5.6	5.8	6.0	6.1	5.7	5.3	5.0
1955	4.9	4.7	4.6	4.7	4.3	4.2	4.0	4.2	4.1	4.3	4.2	4.2
1956	4.0	3.9	4.2	4.0	4.3	4.3	4.4	4.1	3.9	3.9	4.3	4.2
1957	4.2	3.9	3.7	3.9	4.1	4.3	4.2	4.1	4.4	4.5	5.1	5.2
1958	5.8	6.4	6.7	7.4	7.4	7.3	7.5	7.4	7.1	6.7	6.2	6.2
1959	6.0	5.9	5.6	5.2	5.1	5.0	5.1	5.2	5.5	5.7	5.8	5.3
1960	5.2	4.8	5.4	5.2	5.1	5.4	5.5	5.6	5.5	6.1	6.1	6.6
1961	6.6	6.9	6.9	7.0	7.1	6.9	7.0	6.6	6.7	6.5	6.1	6.0
1962	5.8	5.5	5.6	5.6	5.5	5.5	5.4	5.7	5.6	5.4	5.7	5.5
1963	5.7	5.9	5.7	5.7	5.9	5.6	5.6	5.4	5.5	5.5	5.7	5.5
1964	5.6	5.4	5.4	5.3	5.1	5.2	4.9	5.0	5.1	5.1	4.8	5.0
1965	4.9	5.1	4.7	4.8	4.6	4.6	4.4	4.4	4.3	4.2	4.1	4.0
1966	4.0	3.8	3.8	3.8	3.9	3.8	3.8	3.8	3.7	3.7	3.6	3.8
1967	3.9	3.8	3.8	3.8	3.8	3.9	3.8	3.8	3.8	4.0	3.9	3.8
1968	3.7	3.8	3.7	3.5	3.5	3.7	3.7	3.5	3.4	3.4	3.4	3.4
1969	3.4	3.4	3.4	3.4	3.4	3.5	3.5	3.5	3.7	3.7	3.5	3.5
1970	3.9	4.2	4.4	4.6	4.8	4.9	5.0	5.1	5.4	5.5	5.9	6.1
1971	5.9	5.9	6.0	5.9	5.9	5.9	6.0	6.1	6.0	5.8	6.0	6.0
1972	5.8	5.7	5.8	5.7	5.7	5.7	5.6	5.6	5.5	5.6	5.3	5.2
1973	4.9	5.0	4.9	5.0	4.9	4.9	4.8	4.8	4.8	4.6	4.8	4.9
1974	5.1	5.2	5.1	5.1	5.1	5.4	5.5	5.5	5.9	6.0	6.6	7.2
1975	8.1	8.1	8.6	8.8	9.0	8.8	8.6	8.4	8.4	8.4	8.3	8.2
1976	7.9	7.7	7.6	7.7	7.4	7.6	7.8	7.8	7.6	7.7	7.8	7.8
1977	7.5	7.6	7.4	7.2	7.0	7.2	6.9	7.0	6.8	6.8	6.8	6.4
1978	6.4	6.3	6.3	6.1	6.0	5.9	6.2	5.9	6.0	5.8	5.9	6.0
1979	5.9	5.9	5.8	5.8	5.6	5.7	5.7	6.0	5.9	6.0	5.9	6.0
1980	6.3	6.3	6.3	6.9	7.5	7.6	7.8	7.7	7.5	7.5	7.5	7.2

1981	7.5	7.4	7.4	7.2	7.5	7.5	7.2	7.4	7.6	7.9	8.3	8.5
1982	8.6	8.9	9.0	9.3	9.4	9.6	9.8	9.8	10.1	10.4	10.8	10.8
1983	10.4	10.4	10.3	10.2	10.1	10.1	9.4	9.5	9.2	8.8	8.5	8.3
1984	8.0	7.8	7.8	7.7	7.4	7.2	7.5	7.5	7.3	7.4	7.2	7.3
1985	7.3	7.2	7.2	7.3	7.2	7.4	7.4	7.1	7.1	7.1	7.0	7.0
1986	6.7	7.2	7.2	7.1	7.2	7.2	7.0	6.9	7.0	7.0	6.9	6.6
1987	6.6	6.6	6.6	6.3	6.3	6.2	6.1	6.0	5.9	6.0	5.8	5.7
1988	5.7	5.7	5.7	5.4	5.6	5.4	5.4	5.6	5.4	5.4	5.3	5.3
1989	5.4	5.2	5.0	5.2	5.2	5.3	5.2	5.2	5.3	5.3	5.4	5.4
1990	5.4	5.3	5.2	5.4	5.4	5.2	5.5	5.7	5.9	5.9	6.2	6.3
1991	6.4	6.6	6.8	6.7	6.9	6.9	6.8	6.9	6.9	7.0	7.0	7.3
1992	7.3	7.4	7.4	7.4	7.6	7.8	7.7	7.6	7.6	7.3	7.4	7.4
1993	7.3	7.1	7.0	7.1	7.1	7.0	6.9	6.8	6.7	6.8	6.6	6.5
1994	6.6	6.6	6.5	6.4	6.1	6.1	6.1	6.0	5.9	5.8	5.6	5.5
1995	5.6	5.4	5.4	5.8	5.6	5.6	5.7	5.7	5.6	5.5	5.6	5.6
1996	5.6	5.5	5.5	5.6	5.6	5.3	5.5	5.1	5.2	5.2	5.4	5.4
1997	5.3	5.2	5.2	5.1	4.9	5.0	4.9	4.8	4.9	4.7	4.6	4.7
1998	4.6	4.6	4.7	4.3	4.4	4.5	4.5	4.5	4.6	4.5	4.4	4.4
1999	4.3	4.4	4.2	4.3	4.2	4.3	4.3	4.2	4.2	4.1	4.1	4.0
2000	4.0	4.1	4.0	3.8	4.0	4.0	4.0	4.1	3.9	3.9	3.9	3.9
2001	4.2	4.2	4.3	4.4	4.3	4.5	4.6	4.9	5.0	5.3	5.5	5.7
2002	5.7	5.7	5.7	5.9	5.8	5.8	5.8	5.7	5.7	5.7	5.9	6.0
2003	5.8	5.9	5.9	6.0	6.1	6.3	6.2	6.1	6.1	6.0	5.8	5.7
2004	5.7	5.6	5.8	5.6	5.6	5.6	5.5	5.4	5.4	5.5	5.4	5.4
2005	5.3	5.4	5.2	5.2	5.1	5.0	5.0	4.9	5.0	5.0	5.0	4.9
2006	4.7	4.8	4.7	4.7	4.6	4.6	4.7	4.7	4.5	4.4	4.5	4.4
2007	4.6	4.5	4.4	4.5	4.4	4.6	4.7	4.6	4.7	4.7	4.7	5.0
2008	5.0	4.9	5.1	5.0	5.4	5.6	5.8	6.1	6.1	6.5	6.8	7.3
2009	7.8	8.3	8.7	9.0	9.4	9.5	9.5	9.6	9.8	10.0	9.9	9.9
2010	9.8	9.8	9.9	9.9	9.6	9.4	9.4	9.5	9.5	9.4	9.8	9.3
2011	9.1	9.0	9.0	9.1	9.0	9.1	9.0	9.0	9.0	8.8	8.6	8.5
2012	8.3	8.3	8.2	8.2	8.2	8.2	8.2	8.1	7.8	7.8	7.7	7.9
2013	8.0	7.7	7.5	7.6	7.5	7.5	7.3	7.2	7.2	7.2	6.9	6.7
2014	6.6	6.7	6.7	6.2	6.3	6.1	6.2	6.1	5.9	5.7	5.8	5.6
2015	5.7	5.5	5.4	5.4	5.6	5.3	5.2	5.1	5.0	5.0	5.1	5.0

2016	4.8	4.9	5.0	5.1	4.8	4.9	4.8	4.9	5.0	4.9	4.7	4.7
2017	4.7	4.6	4.4	4.5	4.4	4.3	4.3	4.4	4.2	4.1	4.2	4.1
2018	4.0	4.1	4.0	4.0	3.8	4.0	3.8	3.8	3.7	3.8	3.8	3.9
2019	4.0	3.8	3.8	3.7	3.7	3.6	3.6	3.7	3.5	3.6	3.6	3.6
2020	3.5	3.5	4.4	14.8	13.3	11.1	10.2	8.4	7.8	6.9	6.7	6.7
2021	6.3	6.2	6.0	6.1	5.8	5.9	5.4	5.2	4.8	4.6	4.2	

Source: Bureau of Labor Statistics Official Website

https://data.bls.gov/timeseries/LNS14000000?years_option=all_years

ABOUT THE AUTHOR

Tom Mullen hosts the *Tom Mullen Talks Freedom* podcast and is the author of *An Anti-State Christmas, Where Do Conservatives and Liberals Come From? And What Ever Happened to Life, Liberty, and the Pursuit of Happiness?* and *A Return to Common Sense: Reawakening Liberty in the Inhabitants of America.* His writing has been featured in Newsweek, The Huffington Post, The Washington Times, RealClear Markets, LewRockwell.com, and The Foundation for Economic Education. His podcast episodes and writing can be found at www.tommullentalksfreedom.com.

Notes

Chapter 1 Why Elections Haven't Mattered

[1] Tom Mullen. "Commentary: It's the Fed, Stupid!" *WBFO/NPR*, February 12, 2008. https://www.wbfo.org/2008-02-12/commentary-its-the-fed-stupid

[2] Chris McGreal. "Rick Perry attacks Ben Bernanke's 'treasonous' Federal Reserve strategy." *The Guardian*, August 16, 2011. https://www.theguardian.com/world/2011/aug/16/rick-perry-ben-bernanke-treasonous

[3] "Historical Debt Outstanding - Annual 2000 – 2021." *Treasurydirect.gov*. https://www.treasurydirect.gov/govt/reports/pd/histdebt/histdebt_histo5.htm

[4] Alexandra Jaffe. "Biden signs $768.2 billion defense spending bill into law." *ABC News*, December 28, 2021. https://abcnews.go.com/Politics/wireStory/biden-signs-7682-billion-defense-spending-bill-law-81961864

[5] *GlobalFirepower.com*. https://www.globalfirepower.com/defense-spending-budget.php

Chapter 3 What About the Trump Boom?

[1] Jana Kasperkevic. "The US Federal Reserve has created a 'false economy', Trump says." *The Guardian*, September, 6, 2016. https://www.theguardian.com/business/2016/sep/06/trump-us-federal-reserve-false-economy-interest-rates

[2] Ibid

[3] Bob Bryan. "Trump cheers stock market's 'longest winning streak in decades'." *Yahoo Finance*, February 16, 2017. https://finance.yahoo.com/news/trump-cheers-stock-markets-longest-131000075.html

[4] "Open Market Operations." *Federal Reserve Official Website*. https://www.federalreserve.gov/monetarypolicy/openmarket.htm

[5] Heather Long. "Stock market selloff: Just how bad is it?" *CNN Business*, January 4, 2016. https://money.cnn.com/2016/01/04/investing/stocks-market-dow-selloff/index.html

[6] Alexander Saeedy. "Why the Repo Market Is Such a Big Deal—and Why Its $400 Billion Bailout Is So Unnerving." *Fortune*, September 23, 2019. https://fortune.com/2019/09/23/repo-market-big-deal-400-billion-bailout-unnerving/

[7] "Historical Tables." *White House Office of Management and Budget* https://view.officeapps.live.com/op/view.aspx?src=https%3A%2F%2Fwww.whitehouse.gov%2Fwp-content%2Fuploads%2F2021%2F05%2Fhist01z1_fy22.xlsx&wdOrigin=BROWSELINK

Chapter 4 Why Aren't Prices Falling?

[1] "Taking the Measure of Prices and Inflation." *Federal Reserve Bank of Minneapolis*, December 21, 2011. https://www.minneapolisfed.org/article/2011/taking-the-measure-of-prices-and-inflation
[2] James Sherk. "Technology Explains Drop in Manufacturing Jobs." *The Heritage Foundation*, October 12, 2010. https://www.heritage.org/jobs-and-labor/report/technology-explains-drop-manufacturing-jobs
[3] Deirdre McCloskey. "The Myth of Technological Unemployment." *Reason*, August/September 2017. https://reason.com/2017/07/11/the-myth-of-technological-unem/
[4] Stephen McBride. "Baby boomers are retiring — and it's going to have a huge impact on the economy." *Business Insider*, September 4, 2017. https://www.businessinsider.com/impact-of-baby-boomers-retiring-on-the-economy-and-stocks-2017-9
[5] Richard J. Carroll. "Don't Be Shocked If Trump's Economy Goes the Way of Bush's." *Bloomberg*, May 3, 2019. https://www.bloomberg.com/opinion/articles/2019-05-03/trump-s-economy-could-mimic-george-w-bush-s

Chapter 7 OWS and the Tea Party: In the Ballpark But Haven't Found Their Seats
[1] Bill Bonner. "Misguided by Higher Education." *Daily Reckoning*, October 28, 2011. https://dailyreckoning.com/misguided-by-higher-education/

Chapter 9 The Catalyst, Not the Cause
[1] Paul, Ron *The Revolution: A Manifesto* Grand Central Publishing New York, NY 2008 pg. 142

Chapter 11 No One Really Believes the Federal Reserve
[1] "Labor Force Statistics from the Current Population Survey." *U.S. Bureau of Labor Statistics*. https://data.bls.gov/timeseries/LNS14000000
[2] "Consumer Price Index News Release." *U.S. Bureau of Labor Statistics*, March 24, 2015. https://www.bls.gov/news.release/archives/cpi_03242015.htm
[3] "Oil gluts, Great Depression style." *The Economist*, December 30, 2014. https://www.economist.com/news/2014/12/30/oil-gluts-great-depression-style

Chapter 13 Everyone Should Want to End the Fed
[1] Angie Grandstaff. "Moving On Up: 5 Amazing Female Businesses in 19th Century America." *History is Now Magazine*. http://www.historyisnowmagazine.com/blog/2021/7/8/moving-on-up-5-amazing-female-businesses-in-19th-century-america
[2] Emmanuel Saez, Gabriel Zucman. "Wealth Inequality in the United States Since 1913: Evidence from Capitalized Income Tax Data. *National Bureau of Economic Research*, October 2014.

---

[3] Heather Long. "Trump has officially put more tariffs on U.S. allies than on China." *The Washington Post*, May 31, 2018. https://www.washingtonpost.com/news/wonk/wp/2018/05/31/trump-has-officially-put-more-tariffs-on-u-s-allies-than-on-china/

[4] Jeff Mason, Yawen Chen. "China, U.S. agree tariff rollback if phase one trade deal is completed." *Reuters*, November 7, 2019. https://www.reuters.com/article/us-usa-china-trade-idUSKBN1XH0TG

[5] "Rebalancing US-China Trade." *US Trade Representative website*. https://ustr.gov/phase-one

[6] Adam Smith. *An Inquiry into the Nature and Causes of the Wealth of Nations by Adam Smith* (Unexpurgated Edition) (Halcyon Classics) Book IV Chapter III Part II.

[7] "2019 Trade Gap is $616.8 Billion." U.S. Bureau of Economic Analysis. https://www.bea.gov/news/blog/2020-02-05/2019-trade-gap-6168-billion

[8] Ron Paul. "Ron Paul on Afghanistan, U.S. House Floor, 03/17/11." Campaign for Liberty You Tube Channel. https://www.youtube.com/watch?v=GrHm4phj5RQ

[9] Ron Paul. "What We Have Learned From Afghanistan." *Antiwar.com*, June 24, 2013. https://original.antiwar.com/paul/2013/06/23/what-we-have-learned-from-afghanistan/

[10] "Coinage Act of April 2, 1792." *U.S. Mint website*. https://www.usmint.gov/learn/history/historical-documents/coinage-act-of-april-2-1792

[11] Robert Murphy. "Ep. 212 The "Nixon Shock" Was Only the Final Nail in the Coffin of the Gold Dollar." *The Bob Murphy Show*, August 24, 2021. https://www.bobmurphyshow.com/episodes/ep-212-the-nixon-shock-was-only-the-final-nail-in-the-coffin-of-the-gold-dollar/

[12] Kevin R.C. Gutzman. *The Politically Incorrect Guide to the Constitution*. Regnery Publishing, 2007. Pg. 91.

Made in the USA
Monee, IL
08 November 2026

67380041R00104